MW00993723

GREAT
GEORGIAN HOUSES
of AMERICA

Photograph by Edward Pierrepont Beckwith

ENTRANCE FAÇADE, HYDE HALL, COOPERSTOWN, N. Y.

GREAT
GEORGIAN HOUSES
of AMERICA

Published *for the* Benefit

of the

ARCHITECTS' EMERGENCY COMMITTEE

by the

EDITORIAL COMMITTEE

and the

PUBLICATION COMMITTEE

in two volumes

VOLUME I

DOVER PUBLICATIONS, INC., NEW YORK

Published in Canada by General Publishing Company, Ltd., 30 Lesmill Road, Don Mills, Toronto, Ontario.

This Dover edition, first published in 1970, is an unabridged republication of the work originally published by The Editorial Committee of The Great Georgian Houses of America for the benefit of The Architects' Emergency Committee, and printed as follows: Volume I in 1933 by The Kalkhoff Press, Inc., New York; Volume II in 1937 by The Scribner Press, New York.

Standard Book Number: 486-22491-0
Library of Congress Catalog Card Number: 71-105663

Manufactured in the United States of America
Dover Publications, Inc.
180 Varick Street
New York, N.Y. 10014

TABLE OF CONTENTS

ACKNOWLEDGMENTS

THE Editorial Committee takes this opportunity of thanking the owners of the houses illustrated, for their unfailing kindness, courtesy and assistance in obtaining the data used in the preparation of the book. Thanks are due particularly to *Frank Whitney, Esq.*, of the HERMITAGE; the *Misses Frost* of the MILES BREWTON HOUSE; *Mrs. George Washington Roebling* of the WILLIAM GIBBES HOUSE; *Charles Drayton, Esq.*, of DRAYTON HALL; *W. H. Tayloe, Esq.*, and the *Misses Tayloe* of MOUNT AIRY; *Richard Crane, Esq.*, of WESTOVER; *Mrs. William Eustis* of OATLANDS; *Mrs. Forney Johnston* of BREMO; *Robert Daniels, Esq.*, of BRANDON; *Philip A. Carroll, Esq.*, of DOUGHOREGAN MANOR; *The Honorable Breckenridge Long* of MONTPELIER; *Captain John Ridgely* of HAMPTON; *Miss Sinkler* of THE HIGHLANDS; *Mrs. Bayard Stockton* of MORVEN; *George Hyde Clarke, Esq.*, of HYDE HALL; *T. M. Russell, Esq.*, of the RUSSELL HOUSE; *Mrs. Francis G. Ingersoll* of the CHAMPION HOUSE; *Lathrop Brown, Esq.*, of the HARRISON GRAY OTIS HOUSE; *Mrs. Arthur Lyman* of the LYMAN HOUSE; *John Nicholas Brown, Esq.*, of the NIGHTINGALE HOUSE; *Mrs. Lovell Hodge* of the LADY PEPPERELL HOUSE.

THE Editorial Committee also wishes to express its gratitude to the following societies for their gracious permission to include the houses owned and preserved by them; to the *Ladies' Association* of MOUNT VERNON, who have permitted the measuring, drawing and publication of MOUNT VERNON for the first time in its history; the *Robert E. Lee Memorial Foundation* for STRATFORD; the *Society of Colonial Dames* for their National Clubhouse, DUMBARTON HOUSE in Washington; the *Pennsylvania Art Museum* for MOUNT PLEASANT; to *Mr. Walter Siples*, Curator of the Cincinnati Museum for the TAFT HOUSE; the *Metropolitan Museum of New York City* for information on the VAN RENSSELAER MANOR HOUSE of Albany; the *Philipse Hall Committee* of Yonkers; to *William Sumner Appleton, Esq.*, of the *Society for the Preservation of New England Antiquities* for the HARRISON GRAY OTIS HOUSE; to the *New Hampshire Society of Colonial Dames* who have permitted the first publication of the MOFFATT-LADD HOUSE at Portsmouth, New Hampshire; the *Sweat Memorial Museum* at Portland, Maine; *The Williamsburg Holding Corporation* for their courtesy in making available the drawing of the garden plan of WESTOVER, measured by *Mr. Arthur Shurcliff*; the *Kenmore Association*; the *Waltham Golf Club* for the GOVERNOR GORE HOUSE; the *Marblehead Historical Society* for the LEE HOUSE and the *University of Vermont* for GRASSE MOUNT.

THE Editorial Committee also wishes to express its gratitude for invaluable assistance rendered by *Mr. Albert Simons* of Charleston, who has given freely of his time and loaned material which will be published later in "The Plantation Houses of South Carolina" and to *Mr. William Emerson*, the patron of that publication, and the *Philadelphia Chapter of the American Institute of Architects* and *Harold D. Eberlein, John B. Sinkler, Sidney E. Martin, Philip B. Walls, Morley J. Williams* and *E. H. Pederson*, in supplying drawings and photographs of MOUNT PLEASANT, the HIGHLANDS and the WOODLANDS, in or near Philadelphia, and who are using this material in their publications "Schuylkill River Houses" and "Old Philadelphia" which are in the course of preparation and partly published.

THIS Committee wishes to thank the following for their active and valuable collaboration in the preparation of the material and the details of the publication of the book: *Mrs. Fairfax Harrison, Miss Annie Burr Jennings, Mrs. Luke Vincent Lockwood, Mrs. Charles Andrews, Mrs. Stephen P. Bonsal, Col. H. H. Dodge* of Mount Vernon, *Professor Edmund S. Campbell* of the University of Virginia, *Messrs. Norman Isham, J. Frederick Kelly, George Dudley Seymour, Charles O. Cornelius, Henry Oothout Milliken, Philip Schutze, William McK. Bowman, Horace W. Peaslee, F. W. Kehoe* of the University of Vermont, *Frederick Ellis Jackson, Christopher D. Dutra, Arthur C. Haskell, Channing W. Porter, W. R. Greeley* and *C. J. White*, the *Treasurer of this Committee*.

THIS Committee particularly wishes to thank the Committee of Baltimore architects, composed of *Messrs. Lawrence Hall Fowler, John H. Scarff, George Corner Fenhagen, Dana Loomis, Bayard Turnbull* and *H. McLane Fisher* for their invaluable assistance in collecting data and taking measurements of the Maryland group of houses; and *Mr. John P. Thomas* in collecting data on the SWEAT HOUSE at Portland, Maine.

THE Committee also particularly wishes to thank *Mr. Chester B. Price*, who has spent much time and effort in criticizing the presentation of the drawings.

DWIGHT JAMES BAUM, RICHARD H. DANA, WILLIAM EMERSON, PHILIP L. GOODWIN, R. T. H. HALSEY,
JOHN MEAD HOWELLS, FISKE KIMBALL, EVERETT V. MEEKS, JULIAN PEABODY,
LAWRENCE GRANT WHITE, RUSSELL F. WHITEHEAD
WILLIAM LAWRENCE BOTTOMLEY, *Chairman*

LIST OF SUBSCRIBERS TO
"GREAT GEORGIAN HOUSES OF AMERICA"

THE PRESIDENT OF THE UNITED STATES

Abbott, Gordon
Ackerman, Arthur & Sons
Adams, F. B.
Addison Gallery of American Art
Adler, Miss Blanche
Adler, David
Aldrich, Mrs. Winthrop W.
Alexandre, Mrs. J. H., Sr.
Alger, Mrs. Russell A.
Allen, Mrs. Frederick
Altschul, Mrs. Frank
American Gallery of Art
Appleget, Thomas B.
Artley, W. H.
Astor, Mrs. Vincent
Auchincloss, Charles C.
Auchincloss, Mrs. Hugh D.
Auerbach, Mrs. John Hone
Ayer, Charles F.
Ayer, W. B.

Babcock, Mrs. Richard
Babcock, Mrs. Woodward
Bacon, Mrs. Robert
Bailey, Theodore L.
Baker, Mrs. George F.
Ball, Thomas Ryan
Barclay, H. W.
Barnes, Charles D.
Barnes, Miss Gertrude L.
Bartlett, Mrs. Philip G.
Bartol, Mrs. Henry G.
Beach, Mrs. T. Belknap
Berger, D. Spencer
Berrien, Mrs. Frank D.
Berwind, Mrs. John E.
Berwind, Miss Julia
Bigelow, Mrs. Ruth Campbell
Black & Boyd Mfg. Co.
Blow, George Waller
Bodman, Herbert L.
Boltimore, Mrs. W. G.
Bonsal, Mrs. Stephen
Booker, Mrs. N. J.
Boston Public Library
Bostwick, Dunbar W.
Bottomley, Mrs. W. L.
Bottomley, William Lawrence
Bozart Crafts, Inc.
Bradley, Edson
Branch, Miss Effie K.
Branch, Mrs. John Kerr
Brewster, Mrs. Frederick F.
Brewster, Mrs. Robert S.
Brixey, Mrs. Richard
Bronson, Mrs. J. Hobart
Brooklyn Museum Library
Brown, Mrs. Donaldson
Brown, Mrs. John Nicholas
Brown, Mrs. Lathrop
Bruce, David K. E.
Bruce, Mrs. William Cabell
Buck, Mrs. C. Douglass
Bucknall, Mrs. Henry W. J.
Bulkley, Mrs. Jonathan
Burden, Mrs. James A.
Burden, William A. M.

Burlingame, Mrs. Frederic A.
Burlingham, Charles C.
Burnham Library
Byrne, Miss Phyllis

Cabell, Mrs. Robert G., III
Caldwell, Edward F. & Co.
California Palace of the Legion of Honor
Callais, John
Camp, Mrs. Frederic E.
Cannon, Mrs. Henry White
Carle, Robert W.
Carnegie Library
Carrere, Miss Anna Merven
Cary, Mrs. Guy
Casey, Edward
Castle, W. R.
Century Association
Chadwick, Mrs. E. Gerry
Chase, Miss Edith M.
Chicago Historical Society
Chicago Public Library
Choate, Mrs. Arthur Osgood
Choate, Miss Mabel
City Library of Manchester
Claiborne & Taylor, Inc.
Clark, Gaylord Lee
Clark, Mrs. Julian B.
Clark, Mrs. Stephen H.
Clarke, George Hyde
Cleveland Museum of Art
Cluett, Mrs. G. G.
Cochran, Mrs. Edwin P.
Cochran, Mrs. William F.
Codman, Ogden
Coe, W. R.
Coggeshall, Miss Mary
Colean, Miles L.
Collins, Fletcher
Columbia University Library
Cooke, Mrs. Richard A.
Coolidge, T. J., Jr.
Copeland, Lammot du Pont
Cornell University Library
Corning, Miss Anne
Cox, Attilla
Crane, Donald F.
Cravath, Paul D.
Crisp, H. G. & T. R. Edmunds, Jr.
Crocker, Frank L.
Cromwell, Mrs. Lincoln
Crowninshield, Mrs. F. B.
Cunningham, John, Jr.
Currier Gallery of Art
Cushing, Mrs. Charles
Cushing, Miss Margaret W.
Cutting, Mrs. W. Bayard

Dalton, Robert
Dana, Mrs. R. H.
Danforth, Mrs. Murray S.
Daniel, Robert
D'Arcy, Mrs. Paul
David, Donald K.
Davie, Mrs. Preston
Davis, Walter G.

Davison, Mrs. Henry P.
DeBevoise, George
DeCuevas, George
DeForest, Henry W.
DeLagerberg, Guy
Delano & Aldrich
Delehanty, J. Bradley
Dixon, W. Palmer
Dodge, Donald D.
Donaldson, Mrs. John W.
Dunbaugh, George J.
du Pont, Mrs. Alfred I.
Duveen Bros., Inc.

Edey, Miss Louise
Edmonds, Mrs. John Worth
Elkins, W. M.
Ellis, Mrs. Ralph
Ellsworth, Mrs. J. Magee
Elton, John P.
Ely, Albert H., Jr.
Ely, Wilson C.
Endicott, Mr. & Mrs. Wm. C.
Ensign, Mrs. Joseph P.
Eustis, Mrs. W. C.
Evans, Mrs. Henry
Ewing, William

Falk, Myron S.
Farnam, Mrs. Tracy
Farr, Daniel H. Company
Farrand, Max
Ferry, Mrs. M.
Ferry, Mrs. Ronald M.
Field, Mrs. E. Marshall
Fisher, D. K. Este
Fisher, Samuel H.
Fisher, Mrs. Wm. A.
Flagler, H. H.
Ford Motor Company Library
Fosdick, Raymond B.
Fowler, Laurence Hall
Francis, Mrs. G. Gaffan
Franklin, Mrs. George S.
Freedlander, Joseph R.
Frelinghuysen, P. H. B.
French & Co.
Frick, Miss Anne T.
Frick, Mrs. Childs

Gade, Mrs. John A.
Gallatin, Albert Eugene
Gates, Mrs. A. L.
Georgia School of Technology
Gibbons, Mrs. John H.
Gibson, Hamilton
Gibson, Harvey D.
Gilbert, S. Parker
Glessner, Mrs. J. G. M.
Goodwin, James L.
Goodwin, Mrs. Josephine J.
Goodwin, Philip L.
Goucher College Library
Gould, Mrs. Edwin
Gould, Miss Mary S.
Grew, Randolph C.
Griffen, F. D.
Griffin, Will W.

Griswold, B. Howell, Jr.

Hagen, Winston H.
Haight, Alton C.
Haight, Mrs. Frederick E.
Hall, Perry E.
Halle, H. J.
Halsey, R. T. H.
Hamilton, Edward P.
Hamilton, John G.
Hamilton, William H.
Hammond, Mrs. John Henry
Hammond, Mrs. Paul
Hampel's Book Shop, Inc.
Haneman, John Theodore
Hardenbergh, Thomas E.
Hardon, Mrs. Henry W.
Harkness, Mrs. Edward
Harlan, Miss Laura
Harris, Mrs. Basil
Harrison, Mrs. Jennie G. D.
Hartford, Mrs. E. V.
Harvard College Library
Harvard Cooperative Society
Haskell, Mrs. J. Amory
Hasslacher, Mrs. George F.
Hawkes, Mrs. Forbes
Hawley, Miss Theodosia deR.
Hay, Mrs. Clarence L.
Hayden, Charles
Hegeman, Miss Annie May
Heller, Robert H.
Henry, Seton
Hepburn, M.P., Patrick Buchan
Herter, Albert
Hewitt, Edward S.
Higgins, Charles H.
Higginson, Margaret G.
Hill, James Jerome Reference Library
Hines, Mrs. Walker D.
Hodgdon, Frederick G.
Holland & White
Holland, Julian
Holmes, Gerald A.
Holmes, Oliver Wendell Library
Hooper, Mrs. Harriet
Hopkins, D. Luke
Hopkins, Mrs. Robert D.
Hornblower, Mrs. George S.
Houghton, Arthur A., Jr.
Houghton, Mrs. Arthur A.
Howard, Mrs. George
Howells, John Mead
Hoyt, Charles B.
Humphrey, Mrs. Lewis C.
Huntington, Henry E. Library
Huszagh, Lyman Peyton
Hutcheson, William A.
Hutchins, Mrs. Edward
Hyde, Mrs. Louis F.

Indiana State Library
Ingraham, Edward
Iselin, Miss Louise M.
Iselin, Mrs. O'Donnell
Isham, Norman M.

Jackson, Mrs. Percy
James, Mrs. Bayard
James, Mrs. Oliver B.
Jamison, T. Worth, Jr.
Jarvie, Miss Amelia F. G.
Jennings, Miss Annie Burr
Jennings, Oliver B.
Jensen, William
Johns Hopkins University
Johnson & Faulkner
Johnson, Robert, Jr.
Johnson, Mrs. Robert Wood
Johnson, Mrs. Terrell
Johnston, Mrs. Forney
Johnston, Mrs. Newlands
Jones & Erwin
Jones, Mrs. Marion Telva
Juta, Jan

Kahn, Ely Jacques
Kahn, Mrs. Otto H.
Kalkhoff Press, Inc.
Kean, Mrs. John
Kelley, Mrs. Nicholas
Kennedy, Mrs. J. Foster
Kilbreth, J. William
Kimbel, A. & Sons, Inc.
King, Miss Caroline W.
Kingsbury, Miss Alice E.
Kingsbury, Col. Howard Thayer
Klauser, Miss Cora
Knight, Richard
Knight, Mrs. Webster
Knowlton, Eben B.
Koebler, William G.

Labrot, S. W.
Ladd, Mrs. William S.
Lambert, Gerald B.
Lamhill, Richard V. A.
Lancashire, Mrs. J. Henry
Landon, Harold M.
Landsman, Samuel
Langdon, Miss Helen
Lanier, Mrs. Charles D.
Lashin, Nathan A.
Lee, Arthur H. & Sons, Inc.
Lee, Cazenove G., Jr.
Lefferts, Mrs. Barent
Leidy, Mrs. C. F.
Levi, Julian Clarence
Levy, Isaac M.
Lewis, Wadsworth R.
Lindsay, Sir Ronald and Lady
Littlejohn, Mrs. Robert M.
Lloyd, Mrs. Horatio G.
Lloyd-Smith, Mrs. Wilton
Lockwood, Luke Vincent
Long, Mrs. Breckenridge
Lopez, Mrs. J. E.
Lounsberry, Miss Alice
Low, Mrs. Ethelbert I.
Ludowici-Celadon Co.
Lyman, Miss Mabel
Lyon, Charles Woolsey

McKim, Mead & White
McLane, Mrs. Allan, Jr.
McMillen, Inc.
McWilliam, William
Marburg, Miss Emma
Marsalis, Mrs. Thomas
Marsh, Miss E. Mabel
Mason, Eugene Waterman
Massie, Mrs. William
Mathews, Edward J.

Maxwell, Miss J. Alice
Maynard, Mrs. Walter E.
Melcher, Mrs. Gari
Meltzer, Herman
Mercer, Mrs. William E.
Merle-Smith, Mrs. Kate F.
Merrell, Miss Elenor
Metcalf, Mrs. Jesse H.
Metropolitan Museum of Art
Mettee & Company
Meyer, Eugene
Milbank, Mrs. Jeremiah
Miller, Edgar G., Jr.
Milliken, H. Oothout
Moffatt, Frank Everest, Inc.
Moffatt, R. Burnham
Monroe, Mrs. Robert G.
Moore, Benjamin
Moore, Mrs. Edward S.
Moore, Frederic P.
Moore, Mrs. Paul
Morawetz, Victor
Morgan, Mrs. Henry D.
Morgan, John H.
Morgan, Junius S.
Morgan, Mrs. Junius S.
Morgan, Lancaster
Morgan, Shirley W.
Morgan, William Fellowes
Morris, B. W.
Morris, Mrs. Lewis W.
Morrow, Mrs. Dwight W.
Morss, Mrs. Everett
Moseley, F. S., Jr.
Munson, Mrs. Charles S.

Nash, Mrs. Ogden
Nauman, Spencer G.
Newhall, Thomas
Newton, Francis
Nichols, Mrs. Acosta
Nichols, Mrs. George
Noland, Miss Charlotte H.
Norton, Mrs. C. D.
Norton, Mrs. G. W.
Norton, L. A.
Noyes, Laurence G.
Noyes, Mrs. R. B.

Oberlin College
O'Dwyer, David W.
Olds, Irving S.
Osborn, William Church
Ostrander & Eshleman

Parks, Mrs. Elton
Paskus, Mrs. Benjamin G.
Patterson, Jefferson
Patterson, Mrs. J. M.
Payne, Dr. Bruce R.
Payson, Mrs. Charles S.
Payson, Herbert
Peabody, Julian
Peabody, Wilson & Brown
Peacock, Elizabeth H., Inc.
Pell, Mrs. Stephen H.
Pennoyer, Mrs. Paul G.
Pennsylvania, University of
Perry, Shaw & Hepburn
Peters, Miss Isabel
Peyton, Mrs. William C.
Philadelphia, Free Library of
Phillips, James Duncan
Phillips, William
Phipps, Howard
Phipps, John

Pierrepont, Mrs. Seth
Pinchot, Mrs. Gifford
Pope, John Russell
Pope, Lester B.
Potter, R. Burnside
Pratt, Frederic R.
Pratt, Frederick B.
Pratt, Mrs. Frederick B.
Pratt, George D.
Pratt Institute Free Library
Prentice, Mrs. John H.
Princeton University Library
Pringle & Smith
Providence Athenaeum
Provost, Frederick

Rafferty, Mrs. M. G.
Rawson, Mrs. Hobart
Redmond, Mrs. Johnston L.
Reed, Mr. and Mrs. Vernon
Remington, Norman Co.
Rennie, Miss Louise
Rennolds, Edmund Addison
Rentschler, Mrs. Gordon S.
Reynolds, Mrs. Jackson R.
Reynolds, Mrs. John
Richards, George Huntington
Richardson, George W.
Riddle, Mrs. Theodate Pope
Riley, Miss Mabel L.
Rinschede, Charles A. W.
Robinson, Mrs. Douglas
Robinson, Mrs. Edward
Rockefeller, Mrs. John D., Jr.
Rockefeller, Nelson A.
Roebling, Mrs. W. A.
Rogers, James Gamble
Royal Institute of British
   Architects
Russell, Charles H.
Russell, Faris R.
Russell, T. M.

Saint Margaret's School
Salvage, Samuel A.
Schloesing, Jean
Schmidlapp, Mrs. C. J.
Schofield, Mrs. William H.
Schwab, Miss Katherine P.
Sears, Miss Evelyn G.
Sedgwick, Henry R.
Sharpe, Miss Ellen D.
Sharpe, Henry D.
Shaw, Walter K., Jr.
Sheffield, Henry E.
Sloane, John
Smith, Charles C.
Smith, Dr. E. Terry
Spalding, Mrs. Albert
Sprague, Mrs. Isaac
Solley, Mrs. Katherine Lilly
Stechert, G. E. & Co.
Stern, Philip N.
Stevens, Joseph S.
Stewart, J. Adger
Stillman, Miss Charlotte R.
Stillman, Chauncey D.
Stillman, Dr. Edgar
Stout, Andrew V.
Straus, Percy S.
Strawbridge, Mrs. Robert E., Jr.
Stroheim & Romann
Swan, Mrs. Thomas W.

Talbot, J. A.
Tate, Diane & Marian Hall

Tayloe, Miss Estelle
Taylor, Bertrand L., Jr.
Taylor, Henry Osborne
Thatcher, Mrs. Thomas D.
Thedlow, Inc.
Thomas, John P.
Thomas, Miss Mabel L. H.
Thomas, Mrs. Samuel Hinds
Thompson, M. D.
Thornton, Miss Lucille
Thorp, Mrs. J. G.
Thorp, J. H. & Co.
Tiffany, Mrs. Cameron
Torrance, Mrs. Kenneth
Tovell, G. Walter, Inc.
Townsend, James M.
Treadway, Townsend G.
Treanor & Fatio
Tudor, Mrs. Henry D.
Tyler, Victor M.
Tysen, Mrs. K. K.
Tyssowski, Mrs. John

Utica Public Library

Valentine Museum
Van Cleef, Mrs. Henry
Van Name, Miss Theodora
Vauclain, Samuel
Vernay, Arthur S., Inc.
Vickers, Mrs. Reginald J.
Vietor, Mrs. Ernest G.

Wadsworth, Mrs. Lillian
Walker, William H.
Warren, Whitney
Waterbury, Miss Florance
Watson, Thomas J.
Webb, Mrs. J. Watson
Webb, Maurice
Weddell, Alexander Wilbourne
Wendell, Mrs. Barrett
Westport Public Library
White, Cornelius J.
White, J. Du Pratt
White, Mrs. Miles, Jr.
Whitehouse, J. Norman deR.
Whitney, Arthur
Whitney, Mrs. Geoffrey G.
Whitney, Mrs. George
Whitney, Mrs. Howard
Whitney, Miss S. N.
Whittemore, Gertrude B.
Widener, Mrs. George D.
Williams, Mrs. Andrew Murray
Williams, Mrs. George Weems
Williams, Mrs. Harrison
Wilson, Elsie Cobb
Winston, Mrs. Owen
Winthrop, Grenville L.
Winthrop, Mrs. Robert
Wissmann, F. deR.
Wolcott, Mrs. Henry
Woman's Club of Richmond, Va.
Wood, Miss Margaret White
Wood, Mrs. Willis D.
Woolsey, Heathcote M.
Woolsey, Judge John M.
Worthington, Ellicott H.
Wright, Richardson

Yale University
Yeatman, Georgina Pope
Young, Benjamin Swan

Zinn, Mrs. George

Sir Christopher Wren

Sir William Chambers

Inigo Jones

James Stuart

FOREWORD

THE TWO HUNDRED AND SIXTY illustrations and well-made drawings of some of the great Georgian houses of America which compose this volume tell part of the story of our eighteenth-century domestic architecture. More important still they give convincing evidence of the cultural life and appreciation of the beautiful in eighteenth-century America which until recent years has had little general recognition.

FULL OF CHARM as these houses are we must not regard them as masterpieces of architecture, nor must they be compared with the great baronial houses of England and the Continent, the work of the sixteenth, seventeenth and eighteenth-century architects made known to our people in the three large splendid volumes of Colen [sic] Campbell's *Vitruvius Britannicus*, London, 1715-25, of which Benjamin Franklin and Charles Carroll of Carrollton among others had copies. The four folio volumes of Leoni's *Palladio*, London, 1715, also circulated in this country. However, these illustrations of our old mansions will for all time vividly reflect the architectural knowledge and tastes of the original owners. They will also testify to the interest and general understanding of the *Art of Architecture* among our well-to-do people, who naturally patterned their lives as nearly as possible after those in similar circumstances in England, where some knowledge of architecture was deemed an important part of the gentleman's education. It is interesting to note that "Architecture Taught" was at times stressed in the advertisements of our fashionable teachers of painting and drawing.

THIS INTEREST in architecture in eighteenth-century England, *Our Old Home*, as Nathaniel Hawthorne called it, was more than fortunate for us. Its story has not yet been fully told. It would make an interesting chapter in itself, for to this interest many of our finer houses are due. This subject, however, must be dismissed with a statement that the publication of each of the many large sumptuous and expensive architectural books with their hundreds of beautifully engraved plates was only made possible by the hundreds of advance subscriptions from the ladies and gentlemen of high society in England. Most of these volumes are available for study in the Avery Architectural Library of Columbia University, the Print Department of the Metropolitan Museum of Art and the Library of Congress.

THE LISTS of subscribers to these monumental architectural volumes read like a roll of the English Peerage. The members of the Cabinet subscribed freely, as did the high officers of the Army. It was a period when superb collections of porcelains, furniture, plate and paintings formed the background of many an English home. Further proof of this interest in architecture is found on the title pages of some of the less costly architectural volumes. That necessary book, *The Builder's Dictionary or Gentleman's Companion*, 2 Vols., London, 1734, is but one of many evidences that the market for such books was not confined to professional craftsmen. Other publications such as Robert Morris' *Lectures on Architecture*, "Designed as an Agreeable Entertainment for Gentlemen and more Particularly *Useful* to all who Make Architecture or the Polite Arts their Study," London, 1734, and an exquisitely engraved pocket volume, Batty Langley's *The Builder's Benchmate* with one hundred and eighty-four copper-plates "*Written* For the Use of Gentlemen delighting in True Architecture, and for MASTERS and WORKMEN to Draw from and Work after," London, 1757, are but two of many publications which impress upon us the intense interest in architecture among the English gentlemen.

A SIDELIGHT and yet a strong proof of this widespread interest is found in Josiah Wedgwood's putting upon the market basalt portrait busts and basalt and jasperware medallions, shown above, of some of the great English architects whose names were household words. Wedgwood was a great potter and a great salesman who knew his market. Among these portraits was one after Van Dyck of Inigo Jones (1573-1651), the great architect, who built the Banqueting Hall of WHITEHALL, still to be seen in

London, and that of Sir Christopher Wren (1632-1723), who was given his opportunity by the great fire of London in 1666. The half a hundred steeples and cupolas in London designed by Wren find their children in almost every city and hamlet in this country. Wedgwood also made a portrait of James Stuart, whose magnificent volume, *The Antiquities of Athens*, 1762, marked the beginning of our modern study of Grecian architecture, and one in basalt ware of Sir William Chambers (1726-1796), a well-to-do young Englishman who while on a visit to Canton became absorbed in the fascination of Chinese architecture, of which he made many drawings. Chambers on his return home immediately left the sea for the study of architecture. He is held responsible for that craze for Chinese architectural details which for a time threatened to sweep fashionable England off its feet. Evidences of this craze in America are to be seen in GUNSTON HALL and the bedrooms of WHITEHALL. Another Wedgwood plaque is that of Thomas Pitt, an English Amateur, whom Horace Walpole termed his "present architect", when he was doing over part of STRAWBERRY HILL. Thomas Pitt was the nephew of the Earl of Chatham, and one of the numerous members of the House of Commons who vigorously opposed George the Third's American policy.

OF ALL THESE handsome volumes none has left its mark on American architecture more than the superb large folio volume published in London in 1728 which illustrated the early work of James Gibbs (1682-1754). Its publication was made feasible by the enthusiasm for things architectural of four hundred and eighty-one men and women of England whose names are printed on the pages headed "Subscribers". Its well-engraved plates furnished many suggestions to the Philadelphia amateur, Andrew Hamilton, who was responsible for the elaborate plan of our INDEPENDENCE HALL. Its seven large engravings of the

Thomas Pitt

church of ST. MARTIN IN THE FIELDS built by Gibbs in London in 1722 enabled McBean, a Scotchman, the New York builder of ST. PAUL'S CHAPEL, to almost exactly reproduce it in America forty-four years later. Another plate inspired James Hoban, the Irish professional architect, in the making of the design which won him the competition (1792) for the WHITE HOUSE at Washington (*pp. 114-119*). In fact, our landscapes are dotted with the types of the steeples popularized by Wren; sixteen of Gibbs' drawings of which are engraved in his volume. We owe to it also, indirectly but surely, MOUNT VERNON, the seat of General Washington, the remodelling of which by Washington himself was unquestionably influenced by his visits to that superb stone mansion, MOUNT AIRY, Virginia (*pp. 52-59*), on the Northern Neck, just off the highroad oft ridden by the young Virginia colonel on his frequent trips from Mount Vernon to Williamsburg. This may be seen by a comparison of the reproduction of Plate 58 of Gibbs' (*pl. 1*) with that of the southern façade of MOUNT AIRY (*pp. 57-59*).

FROM THESE two plates, Gibbs' "A Design for a Gentleman in Dorsetshire", and that of the southern façade of MOUNT AIRY, we can also obtain a fair idea of how our eighteenth-century gentlemen planned their mansion houses. There was very little slavish copying by our ancestors. We can picture them poring over their architectural volumes, picking out details here and there which pleased their fancies, and instructing their skilled indentured servants or the local master-carpenter, "Undertaker", as he was sometimes called, to incorporate them into the proposed building. Different plates furnished suggestions for the treatment of the other façades as well as the layout of the noble forecourt (*pp. 52-55*) where "The offices are on each Side of the Court having a cover'd Communication from the House by an Arcade." The stone

PLATE 1

A Design for a Gentleman in Dorsetshire from James Gibbs

urns might well have been carved from one of the fifty-four shown in the same volume.

THE EASTERN façade of MOUNT AIRY (*p. 56*), though less monumental, is not less interesting with its Venetian window and arched over window designed closely after those in Plate XLI in Batty Langley's *The City and Country Builder's and Workman's Treasury of Designs*, London, 1739. This book with its one hundred and eighty-six plates and hundreds of details had wide circulation in this country. It was from its Plate LI (*pl. 7*) Washington obtained the details for his fine Venetian window (*p. 76*), and from Plate LIV (*pl. 5*), the elliptical window (*p. 72, 74–75*) in the pediment of the front façade of MOUNT VERNON. The heavy bevelling of the thick pine sheathing at MOUNT VERNON is thoroughly reminiscent of that of the white stone front of MOUNT AIRY and the plate in

Gibbs' Architecture which served as a plan for the latter building.

WE ARE APT to think of Washington only as the great soldier and statesman. He was also his own architect, remodelling with the assistance of trained indentured servant craftsmen the little oblong box left him by his brother into the noble mansion which excited the admiration of his many visitors from abroad. One of them, John Hughes, noted in his diary, 1785, "It is astonishing with what niceness he [Washington] directs everything in the building way, condescending even to measure the things himself, that all may be perfectly uniform." MOUNT VERNON's greatest improvements were under way just when Washington was called to take command of the Army at Cambridge. His letters and journals voice his anxieties that every detail that he had planned be exactly carried out.

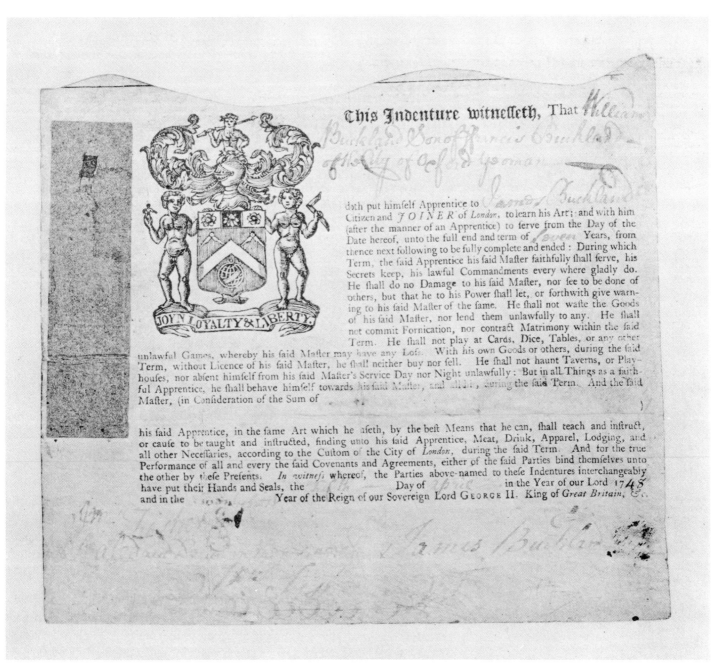

PLATE 2

It is but natural that our earliest houses followed rather closely the lines of those the colonists had left behind them in England. One of the oldest of the houses herein illustrated, STRATFORD HALL (1725-30) (*pp. 46-51*), is of the Elizabethan H-shaped form made popular in England by John Thorpe (1570-1610) and later used so successfully by Inigo Jones. Its ground plan differs but little from that in a plate labelled "A Platform for a Mansion House" which appeared in *The City and Country Purchaser and Builder*, London, 1667, a little pocket volume by Stephen Primat, issued to guide the rebuilding by the many unfortunates who had lost their homes in London's great fire.

As yet we know but little of the history of those many trained workmen, English and native, who assisted our gentlemen in the planning and building of their beautiful homes. Unquestionably many of their stories will be unfolded now that our historians are giving greater recognition to the importance of the cultural development of our people. None of them can have more romance than that of William Buckland (1734-1774), some of whose remarkable work is detailed in *pp. 154-160, 146-153*, of the MATTHIAS HAMMOND house and WHITEHALL at Annapolis. These along with the RIDOUT, SCOTT, BRICE, PACA, and CHASE houses at Annapolis are each of great individuality and charm and form a distinguished group such as no other colonial builder has left behind him. Fortunately it has been possible to unravel Buckland's life story through the coming to light of two important parchments (*pls. 2, 8*), his apprenticeship papers (1748) to his uncle, James Buckland, "Citizen and JOINER" of London, and his four-year indentureship (1755) as "Carpenter and Joiner" to Thomson Mason, who had been studying at the Inner Temple, London, and was returning to Virginia

PLATE 3
House of Joseph Coolidge, Esq., by Bulfinch

PLATE 4
House of Joseph Barrell, Esq., by Bulfinch

bringing a trained craftsman to assist his brother, George Mason, in building his mansion, GUNSTON HALL, on the Potomac. So far his story is but one of many. Southern gentlemen, Washington among them, were wont to send to London for skilled workmen who indentured themselves for a term of years at a wage, in Buckland's case, of twenty pounds a year and with "meat, drink, washing, lodging" and their transportation across the sea provided. On the back of the apprenticeship certificate in Buckland's own handwriting is a brief story of his life. "The within named W. Buckland was born in the Parish of St. Peters-in-the-East in the City of Oxford on the 14th day of August, 1734 and was bound an apprentice to his uncle, James Buckland in London on the 5th day of April, 1748, and came to Virginia with Thomson Mason, Esquire, the 14th day of August, 1755." It is an interesting fact that James Buckland to whom our William Buckland was apprenticed was none other than the James Buckland for fifty years a famous and respected bookseller, "At the Buck in Pater-Noster Row." On the back of the indentureship are a few words written by George Mason to the effect that William Buckland had done all the carpenter's and joiner's work on his elaborate house just completed in Virginia. They allow the deduction that this highly trained twenty-one-year-old young Englishman acted as technical adviser and practical builder, carver, and joiner, to George Mason and that Mason and Buckland with the aid of architectural books drew up the elaborate plan for GUNSTON HALL (*pls. 10-13*). The building is of the rectangular story-and-a-half type characteristic of early eighteenth-century Virginia architecture. However, it is very individualistic. Its extraordinary porches, front and rear, are not found elsewhere in America and its interior woodwork has an enrichment of carved ornament not equalled in any other of the Virginia houses.

PROBABLY NO OTHER indentured servant who came to America had such a background of training for an architect—the first fourteen years spent in the classic shades of Oxford, then seven years in the London home of his uncle, James Buckland (1713-1791), joiner and bookseller. What a chance for an education this apprentice had among

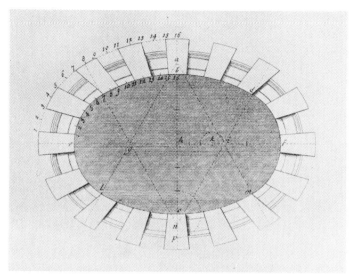

PLATE 5

those well-filled bookshelves! It explains Buckland's familiarity with architectural publications and his very large, for the time, architectural library of seventeen volumes of which his work tells us he constantly made use.

WHERE BUCKLAND obtained his builder's experience we do not know as yet. He may have done some of the joiner's work or had a chance to study carefully that beautiful HONINGTON HALL in Warwickshire, twenty-two miles from Oxford, Buckland's home town—a Charles II house, remodelled just after the middle of the eighteenth century by a wealthy London merchant, Joseph Townsend, and copiously illustrated in Volume V of Tipping's *English Houses*. A glance at the illustrations of HONINGTON HALL shows us the stone quoins, the hexagonal porch with the triglyphs which Buckland used in the frieze below the cornice of the rear porch (*pl. 11*) at GUNSTON HALL, as well as the elaborately carved modillions of the cornices in his SCOTT and CHASE houses and WHITEHALL (*p. 153*) at Annapolis, and the octagonal extension which Buckland used in his addition to OGLE HALL in the same city.

THE MOST ASSURING proof that Buckland must have known HONINGTON HALL is to be seen in the elaborately carved panels of the interior shutters of its oak room, features most unusual if not unique in English houses. Rather similar ones are found in Buckland's MATTHIAS HAMMOND house (*p. 158*), PACA and CHASE houses at Annapolis, but Buckland enriched his with large rosettes in relief in the center of each panel. Other unusual details which strengthen the argument are the highly carved window trim with the same "ribband and flower" carvings in the saloon of HONINGTON HALL which Buckland used at the MATTHIAS HAMMOND house, and the carved shutters and carved flattened consoles of the window trim suggestive of those in the CHASE house. The great doorways in the oak room may have suggested the similar but simplified ones at WHITEHALL. The oak leaves and acorns in the friezes are motifs Buckland used in the PACA house and WHITEHALL (*p. 153*). The carved modillions of the pediment

over the doors of the saloon have the same bands of egg-and-dart and dentil mouldings as those on the great doorways at WHITEHALL (*p. 150*). Another convincing proof of Buckland's knowledge of HONINGTON HALL is the use of masks in the corners of the saloon there. Buckland introduced carved masks in the corners of the coved ceiling at WHITEHALL. The incised line of carved ornament in the center of the doors, themselves, used at HONINGTON HALL is also found in two of Buckland's houses, WHITEHALL and the CHASE HOUSE.

UNQUESTIONABLY BUCKLAND's most individualistic design is that of the front porch of GUNSTON HALL (*pl. 10*), the home of Virginia's great statesman, George Mason, author of the Virginia Bill of Rights, and friend and near neighbor of Washington. GUNSTON HALL is now the cherished home of Louis Hertle who while retaining a life ownership has deeded to the State of Virginia this superb monument of our cultural life of the eighteenth century. Probably the mystery as to what suggested to Buckland and Mason the exact classical lines of this porch will never be solved. They follow exactly those on a rare Roman medal of the Emperor Philip, now in the British Museum, which pictures the TEMPLE OF TYCHE at Eumeneia, Asia Minor. It has only been engraved once, appearing in the elaborate tailpiece of the third chapter of Stuart and Revett's *Antiquities of Athens*, 1762. Perhaps Buckland was shown the medal and heard it discussed by the habitués of the bookshop of his popular uncle-bookseller, who was one of the authorized vendors of the second edition, 1758, of Swan's *The British Architect or The Builder's Treasury*, London, 1745, from which Buckland drew freely for his details. This volume had such popularity in America, especially among Philadelphia artisans, that Robert Bell, "Bookseller, Third-Street, next Door to St. Paul's Church", Phila-

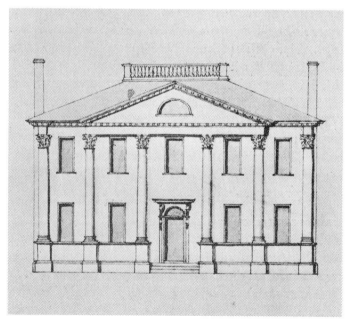

PLATE 6
House of "Doctor" John Joy, by Bulfinch

13

delphia, issued in 1775 a pirated edition of its sixty folio plates. Its list of "Encouragers" gives us the names of sixty master builders and a hundred and ten house carpenters, striking testimony of the interest the Philadelphia men of the building trade had in improving their craftsmanship, the high quality of which is evidenced in the splendid old colonial houses of Philadelphia and vicinity of which MOUNT PLEASANT (*pp. 176-180*) in Fairmount Park is an outstanding example. The influence of Plate LI in the English edition of this book can be seen in the details of the LEE HOUSE (1768) at Marblehead, Massachusetts (*p. 245*).

PLATES XLIX AND L in the same volume gave Washington the designs for the elaborate overmantel bearing his coat of arms in the West Parlor (*p. 82*) and the chimney-piece thus referred to in a paragraph of a letter to his overseer, Lund Washington, dated "Cambridge, Aug. 20, 1775. I wish you would quicken Lamphire and Sears about the Dining Room Chimney Piece (to be executed as mentioned in one of my last letters) as I wish to have that end of the House completely finished before I return." Another extract from the same letter voices Washington's interest in architectural detail. "I wish you had done the end of the New Kitchen next the Garden as also the Old Kitchen with rusticated boards; however, as it is not I would have the Corners done so in the manner of our new Church (those two especially which fronts the Quarters)". He had in mind the quoins on the corners of Pohick Church. Lamphire was evidently a local joiner as we find an entry in one of Washington's account books dated "Aug. 10, 1759—By Going Lamphire in full for Turnery. 7.14.7½", payment probably for the spindles of the staircase (*p. 80*). It was also at this time that the ornamental plaster ceilings of the parlor (*p. 82*) and dining room (*p. 83*) replaced the "papier machee" ornaments Washington had ordered from England in 1757. They are the work of the same Frenchman who did the notable plaster work at KENMORE (*pp. 111-113*), the house of Washington's sister, Betty Lewis. Not until 1786 was Washington able to attend to the finishing of the interior of the "Banquet Room" (*p. 84*) with its ornate plaster work into which instead of the proverbial musical instruments he had inserted hoes, rakes, harrows, etc., emblems of agriculture and therefore peculiarly personal to Washington, the eighteenth-century squire. For this work Washington employed John Rawlins of Baltimore as "undertaker" and Richard Thorpe. Washington notes the latter as "director of the work".

ANOTHER OF THESE architectural books written by Abraham Swan, also in Buckland's library, *The Carpenters Complete Instructor in Several Hundred Designs* (1758), may be held responsible for the design of the enormous dome and cupola of the monumental STATE HOUSE at Annapolis. The octagonal cupola and weather-vane at MOUNT VERNON (*pp. 74-75*) closely followed the lines of one of the eight octagonal cupolas in this same useful vol-

PLATE 7

ume. It is difficult not to believe that Washington when planning the remodelling at MOUNT VERNON in 1775 did not discuss the suggested changes with Buckland, whom he must have known when the neighboring GUNSTON HALL was in process of erection, for Washington made many lengthy visits to Annapolis in 1771, 1772 and 1773.

THE FRONT PARLOR of GUNSTON HALL must have been the last word in America in the new style of architecture over which fashionable England was going wild. Dominating Chinese motifs here are the rows of shark's teeth projecting from the window and door heads, also the diagonal ornaments on the window frames. The latter appear also in the upper part of the window trim in the adjoining parlor (*pl. 13*). Other Chinese motifs are the linked circles on the door heads (*pl. 12*). Probably no early American room has such profusion of ornament. The cabinets flanking the mantelpiece, the elaborately carved chair-rail, the "ribband and flower" ornaments at the bases of the pilasters, and the lavishly carved baseboard mouldings make the room of extraordinary richness. We find the same details here and there in Buckland's Annapolis houses.

GEORGE MASON'S LETTER of endorsement and the fame of the wonder house on which Buckland had worked together with his ability gave him his opportunity in Annapolis, the metropolis of Maryland and a day and a half journey from GUNSTON HALL. During the next ten years we find him and his books responsible for the building of the aforementioned six beautiful houses there. The former

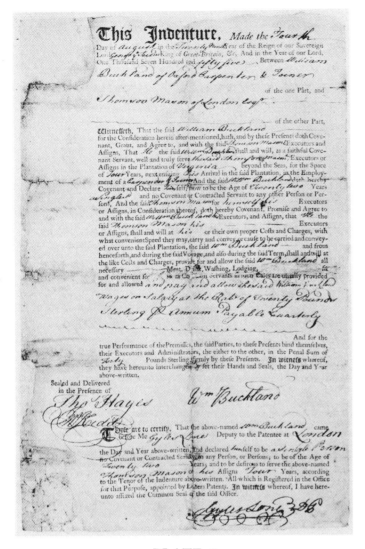

PLATE 8

indentured servant became socially accepted, being noted in a document in 1774 as "William Buckland, Gentleman". The inventory of his estate informs us that he had his own corps of indentured artisans to do his building. His daughter married John Callahan, Register of the Land Office, and his granddaughter, Sarah Callahan, married Richard Harwood, who owned the house that Buckland had built for Matthias Hammond. Buckland's splendid portrait by Charles Willson Peale still hangs there.

THIS HOUSE, the most beautiful town house (*pp. 154–160*) in America, belonging originally to Matthias Hammond, an active Son of Liberty, was only finished shortly before Buckland's death in 1774. No such front doorway (*p. 157*) exists elsewhere on this side of the water. The carvings of the roses and banded laurel are in high relief and heavily undercut. Buckland was a trained carver and owned among other volumes the exquisitely engraved and costly *One Hundred & Fifty New Designs by Thos Johnson, Carver*, London, 1761. His library also contained a copy of Chippendale's *Director*. We know of his having made some furniture.

THE ELABORATE bull's-eye window of the MATTHIAS HAMMOND house (*p. 155*) follows closely the lines of one on Plate 110 of his Gibbs' *Architecture* (*pl. 9*). Most unusual are the "hyphens" which connect the wings to the main house. The same delicate pediments and niches were on the screen at HONINGTON HALL. The delightful octagonal ends of the wings of the façade probably were inspired by Plate 25 in another of Buckland's books, *Select Architecture* by Robert Morris, London, 1751. The main room (*pp. 158-159*), probably the banquet room, baffles all description. Here we see the elaborate inside shutters, a feature of the oak room at HONINGTON HALL. The frieze over the window, as well as that on the doorheads, has the elaborately carved arabesques and eagle's heads so much used by Inigo Jones. They must have been taken from Plate 49, the façade of the King's apartments at WHITEHALL in William Kent's *The Designs of Inigo Jones*, 1727. The extraordinary chair-rail and baseboard with their richness of carving were influenced by the various plates in Swan's *Designs*, 1757. Buckland's baseboards and chair-rails, as he did them in GUNSTON HALL, the MATTHIAS HAMMOND house, the CHASE house, and WHITEHALL, are very different from those put in by his American contemporaries. They project almost four inches from the wall, thereby enabling the elaborately carved mouldings. The design for the upper part of the chair-rail appears in *One Hundred & Fifty New Designs by Thos Johnson*. The door trim (*p. 158*) is equally noteworthy. The beautifully turned bobbins at the end of the acanthus leaves on the consoles which support the door heads are exquisite details. There are Adam touches in the house. Evidently Buckland was quick to adopt any new styles which were becoming popular in London. We find a decided Adam motif in the oblong gouging in the doorways as well as in the beautiful simple frieze of the upstairs ballroom. We also find Adam touches in Buckland's plaster work in the CHASE and PACA houses and at WHITEHALL. The heavy and elaborate cornice of the banquet room (*p. 159*) follows the exact lines of Plate VII in Swan's *British Architect*.

OF EQUAL IMPORTANCE with the MATTHIAS HAMMOND house and one of the noblest of our country mansions of colonial days is WHITEHALL (*pp. 146-153*), built by Governor Horatio Sharpe in 1765-70 upon a point in the Chesapeake a few miles distant from Annapolis. Circumstantial evidence proves that the Governor was his own builder and employed Buckland as the architect. Its bricks were undoubtedly burned on the place, no uncommon practice here as we had our wandering brickmakers, such as one William Vennell, brickmaker, who advertised in the *Maryland Gazette* as "Living *near* Annapolis, Gives this Public Notice, That he will make BRICKS, and Burn them and stand to the Loss, at 2/6 per Thousand, the Employer finding him Provisions and Hands, the Hands to consist of Two Men and Three Boys." The slates for the roofing were slit on the place, and the elaborate wood carvings took years for their completion. Building in those days was a

PLATE 9

long-drawn-out operation, five or six years often elapsing before the houses were ready for occupancy.

THE NORTH FAÇADE (*pp. 148-149*) with its portholes and arches reeks of the architectural atmosphere created by James Gibbs. The steps, however, are of modern construction. The south façade (*p. 146*) is a great achievement. It is the earliest example of the use of the temple form of domestic architecture now standing in America. It may well have been inspired by any of the half a dozen elevations in Buckland's copy of Morris' *Select Architecture.* Though new to America no design could have been more appropriate for the house of a colonial governor. Its type had been selected for the stately MANSION HOUSE of London's Chief Magistrate, completed just before both Sharpe and Buckland had left London. The pediment (*p. 153*) is ornate with its richly carved modillions. The lines of carved mouldings on the frieze are most unusual and follow line for line Plate XXIX of Buckland's expensive elephant folio volumes, *The Perspective of Architecture,* by Joshua Kirby, London, 1761. Its dedication to George the Third tells us: "This Work was Begun by your Majesty's Command, Carried on under your Eye and now Published by your Royal Munificence."

FEATURES OF THE main room are the two tall and richly carved doorways (*p. 150*). The modillions of their pediments are similar but reduced in scale to those in the cornice of the pediment of the portico. Heavily carved Greek frets cover the soffits of the four doorways. No such window trim (*p. 150*) is found in our other houses. Their flattened consoles are suggestive, but of better design than the several engraved in Swan's *Designs.* The lesser doorways (*p. 152*) are heavily loaded with ornament and are decidedly Adam in feeling. Very noteworthy is the introduction of beautifully carved shells

into the bands of egg-and-dart ornament of which Buckland was so fond. The embellishment of the doors must have been influenced by plates in Adam's *Spalatro,* London, 1764, to which Governor Sharpe's patron, "The Honorable Frederick, Lord Baltimore", was a subscriber, or from a plate, Chap. II Pl. VII, in a superb volume, *The Ionian Antiquities,* 1769. The heavy expenses of this publication were defrayed by the Society of Dilettanti, a jovial social club of thirty-four distinguished English gentlemen interested in the Fine Arts, among whom were the brother of Governor Farquier of Virginia, Thomas Jefferson's early mentor in the world of art, and Charles James Fox. In the same volume, Chap. III Pl. VIII, is a detail of the griffins from the TEMPLE OF APOLLO DIDYMAEUS introduced by Jefferson into the friezes of the mantel and cornices of his imposing galleried entrance hall at MONTICELLO (*p. 69*). A unique feature of this princely room at WHITEHALL is the elaborately carved and framed wooden masks inserted into the corners of the coved ceiling (*p. 151*).

THOMAS JEFFERSON, architect and builder of MONTICELLO (*pp. 67-69*) and architect of BREMO (*pp. 92-102*) must have been early influenced by Buckland's work. Among his drawings is a ground plan of the MATTHIAS HAMMOND house made probably when he was spending the winter of 1783-84 at Annapolis. Undoubtedly this house suggested

PLATE 10

16

to him the octagonal ends which he placed on the sides of beautiful MONTICELLO (*p. 68*). It must have been at WHITEHALL that he first saw the temple form of architecture, such an outstanding feature of MONTICELLO. In his college days at William and Mary, Jefferson was fortunate in having free access to the table of Governor Farquier, a cultivated Englishman and Fellow of the Royal Society. It was at these dinners, afterwards wrote Jefferson, "I have heard more good sense, more rational and philosophical conversation than in all my life besides." Authorities agree that it was there that Jefferson first saw those volumes of *Palladio* which opened his vision and stimulated his imagination. They set him dreaming of a beautiful home on his mountain top. One of these volumes furnished him with the plan which while a student he copied for the layout of his future home. He adhered closely to it. The central building he rebuilt after his stay in Paris where he became fascinated with the domed and Doric-porticoed building, the MAISON DE SALM, then in process of building.

THE INTERIOR OF MONTICELLO is full of fascinating classic details culled from Jefferson's enormous architectural library. The most unusual are the friezes of the cornices, doorheads, and mantel of the parlor. He surely took them from one of his Piranesi prints—that of the Roman TEMPLE OF GIOVE TONANTE on which appeared the same combination of shields, ewers, knives, ox-skulls, etc. The blue and white classical plaques inserted in the mantelpiece of the dining-room are apparently the sole survivors of such use of Wedgwood ware in America.

FEW OF THE HOUSES illustrated in this volume are the work of architects who had the advantages of an intensive technical training. The beautiful home of JOSEPH MANIGAULT (*pp. 30-33*) at Charleston, South Carolina, is from plans furnished by his brother, Gabriel, who was educated abroad and like many sons of our well-to-do families had received a certain amount of training in drawing and the fine arts. However, the superb MILES BREWTON house (*pp. 34-38*) in the same city is the work of Ezra Waite, a lately arrived "Civil Architect, House-Builder in general and Carver from London".

PLATE 11

CHARLES CARROLL of CARROLLTON was the builder of HOMEWOOD (c. 1800) (pp. 138-145). His early education in France and England gave him an appreciation of the fine arts and a willingness to defray the ex-

PLATE 12

except about three months of hurried employment, when he was engaged in victualing a French fleet in our harbour, my time passed very idly and I was at leisure to cultivate a taste for Architecture, which was en-

pense of costly HOMEWOOD, now the beautifully furnished museum of Johns Hopkins University. The actual work was done by William Edwards, "house-carpenter at the end of Pratt Street, Baltimore". The delicate gouged ornamentation there must be seen to be fully appreciated. It follows a variation of Adam motifs popularized by William Paine of London (c. 1730-1790), the sixth edition of one of whose books, *The Practical Builder or Workman's General Assistant*, London, 1782, was reproduced in Boston in 1796 and in Philadelphia in 1797 under the title of *The Practical House Carpenter or Youth's Instructor*. Its plates tell us where Charles Carroll plucked the unusual designs for the doorways of the dining-room; also for some of the mantelpieces of the house.

NO MAN HAD A more inspiring influence on New England architecture in the days of the Early Republic than Charles Bulfinch (1763-1844), the architect of the Boston and Hartford State Houses and later successor to Latrobe as architect of the Capitol at Washington. He also designed two fine houses for HARRISON GRAY OTIS (pp. 224-233). One is now the home of The Society for the Preservation of New England Antiquities, which has preserved to us so many of the ancient dwellings in New England. Charles Bulfinch was an American by birth and tradition; he came from a fine Boston family. His father and grandfather were physicians and men of culture and his mother was the daughter of a very wealthy Boston merchant. His autobiography, quoted in *Bulfinch's Life* by his granddaughter, tells us of the beginnings of his interest in architecture. He wrote that after graduating at Harvard in the Class of '81:

"MY DISPOSITION WOULD have led me to the study of Physic, but my father was averse to my engaging in the practice of what he considered a laborious profession & I was placed in the counting room of Joseph Barrell, Esq., an intimate friend & esteemed a correct merchant; but unfortunately the unsettled state of the times prevented Mr. Barrell from engaging in any active business, so that for

couraged by attending to Mr. Barrell's improvements of his estate and [the improvements] on our dwelling house & the houses of some friends, all of which had become exceedingly dilapidated during the war. Coming of age about this time, an Uncle, George Apthorp, died in England, and a portion of his property, about £200 Stlg, came to my parents, who devoted it to my use for a visit to Europe. I accordingly embarked in June, 1785, and returned Jan. 1787."

HIS JOURNEY HAD carried him through France and Italy, the Mecca of the many Englishmen interested in the various phases of art. His own account continues: "This tour was highly gratifying, as you may well suppose. I was delighted in observing the numerous objects & beauties of nature & art that I met with on all sides, particularly the wonders of Architecture, & the kindred arts of painting & sculpture, as my letters to friends at home very fully express; but these pursuits did not confirm me in any business habits of buying & selling, on the contrary they had a powerful adverse influence on my whole after life."

A PARAGRAPH IN another letter which he wrote to his parents from Philadelphia, April 2, 1789, shows his opinion of the grandiose.

"THIS CITY IS NOT much altered since I was last here except in its increase; the same plain style of building is kept up and the same quakerish neatness. One only great exception to this is the house of Mr. Bingham, which is in a style which would be esteemed splendid even in the most luxurious parts of Europe. Elegance of construction; white marble staircase, valuable paintings, the richest furniture and the utmost magnificence of decoration make it a palace in my opinion far *too* rich for *any* man in this country."

BULFINCH'S WORK IS noted for its inherent good taste in architectural details and fine proportions. His early style is well illustrated in his own drawings (*pls. 3-4-6*) of the elevations and important houses given him to build by family friends at almost the outset of his career, 1792. In these we can see Bulfinch's translation of the classic styles

18

of architecture which had impressed him abroad into the simple façades soon to become the vogue in New England. The most elegant of the three, the house of Joseph Barrell, Bulfinch's first employer, has been described in all annals of American architecture. Many of the details so often used by Bulfinch are found in the sole surviving picture of a famous dwelling house on Bowdoin Street, that of Joseph Coolidge, Jr., wealthy Boston merchant and father-in-law of Bulfinch's sister. Surrounded by extensive grounds it has gone down in history as having been considered one of the most beautiful residences in Boston. The third elevation is of another long departed house, that of "Doctor" John Joy, which stood until 1843 on Beacon Street, adjoining the house of John Hancock. On these three drawings are shown the pilasters starting from the second story, the engaged columns, the semi-circular window, so frequently used by Bulfinch, and the tablets over the windows, details found in Bulfinch's carefully executed drawing of Federal Hall done while on a visit to New York to witness the inauguration of President Washington and engraved for the June, 1789, number of the *Massachusetts Magazine*.

ANOTHER NATIVE-BORN architect who left a deep impress upon New England's architectural history was Samuel McIntire (1754-1811) of Salem, Massachusetts, architect and builder, in the last decade of the eighteenth century, of the LYMAN HOUSE (*pp. 238-240*), Waltham, Massachusetts. He was the son of a Salem master-carpenter. The new style of architecture introduced by Bulfinch made a great impression on him. His work became filled with classic details. He apparently made but little use of architectural books though in the advertisement of the sale of his effects in 1811 we find "Paladia Architecture, best kind" among the books offered for sale.

WHILE McINTIRE HAD not the educational advantages enjoyed by Bulfinch, the years of practical training in joinery and wood-carving in his father's shop allowed him to leave behind a group of houses in Salem different from those we find elsewhere. That they had a style of their own is largely due to McIntire's love for wood-carving. His interiors frequently were embellished with his own heavy relief carving of eagles, baskets of fruit, sheaves of wheat, garlands, etc. These were more sturdy in execution and fitting to the New England tradition than the delicate ornaments he used in some of his very elaborate interiors.

MANY OF THE HOUSES of the Hudson River Valley were of great importance. Most imposing was that built by STEPHEN VAN RENSSELAER at Albany in 1765 (*pp. 202-205*), the great hallway of which (*pp. 204-205*) is one of the features of the American Wing of the Metropolitan Museum. Outstanding is the superb archway (*p. 204*) with its heavily undercut spandrels, the design for which was taken from another of the English architectural books to which our architecture is so heavily indebted, *A New*

PLATE 13

Book of Ornaments with Twelve Leaves by M. Lock and H. Copland, London, 1752.

CENTRAL NEW YORK had its finished carpenter-architects. Among others Joseph Hooker (1766-1833), who is responsible for the noble addition of the state dining-room and saloon of the latest of the manor houses, HYDE HALL, (*pp. 196-201*) shown in this volume. This magnificent house on the shores of Otsego Lake, then on the very borders of the wilderness, was built in 1811 and added to in 1833. The design of the elaborate frieze beneath the cornice of the saloon (*p. 200*) is found on Plate 29 of *The American Builder's Companion*, a publication (1806), by a New England architect, Asher Benjamin (1773-1845) and of such popularity that it ran into many editions.

IT HAS BEEN DEEMED advisable that in no way should this brief foreword attempt to cover all the mansions illustrated in this volume, sponsored by the Architects' Emergency Committee. Possibly enough has been said to stimulate the reader to carry on further research along similar lines. No such elaborate illustrations of our Georgian Mansions have hitherto been attempted. Their publication has been made possible by the untiring and unselfish efforts of the members of the Architectural profession, notably Dwight James Baum, William Lawrence Bottomley, chairman, Richard H. Dana, William Emerson, Philip L. Goodwin, John Mead Howells, Fiske Kimball, Everett V. Meeks, Julian Peabody, Lawrence Grant White, and Russell F. Whitehead.

TO OUR ARCHITECTS and their clients throughout this country this work must be invaluable. Now that our colleges and more advanced schools are stressing in their revised curriculums the importance of the study of the Fine Arts its pages must make an especial appeal to the youth of the land as well as to their elders. To all Americans its illustrations will ever be convincing testimony to the skill and taste of our early builders and more important still be a monument to the knowledge and appreciation of good architecture of the men who made our Republic possible and started it on its career at a period when the world was torn up by wars and social upheavals.

R. T. H. Halsey

THE HERMITAGE, SAVANNAH, GEORGIA, ENTRANCE FAÇADE

Entrance Facade

The · Hermitage · Savannah · Georgia

Built and owned by Mr Henry Mc Alpin 1800

graphic scale ⊢——┴——┘ 1/16"=1'0 actual scale

K. Sixty del.

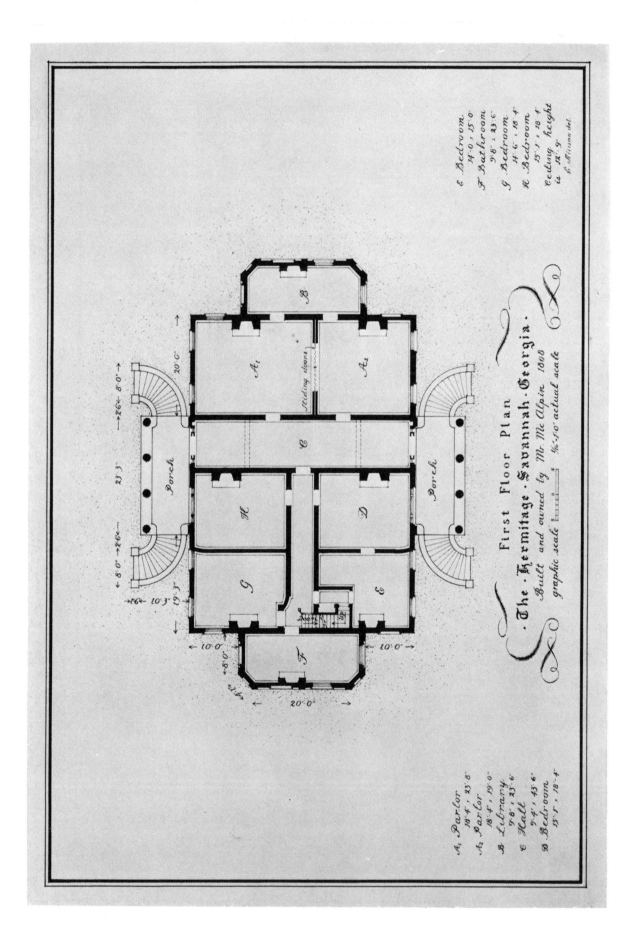

First Floor Plan
· The · Hermitage · Savannah · Georgia ·
Built and owned by Mr. McAlpin 1808
graphic scale   ⅛" = 1'-0" actual scale

A₁ Parlor
    18'-4 × 23'-8
A₂ Parlor
    18'-4 × 19'-0
B Library
    9'-8 × 23'-6
C Hall
    9'-4 × 43'-6
D Bedroom
    15'-1 × 18'-4

E Bedroom
    14'-0 × 15'-0
F Bathroom
    9'-8 × 13'-6
G Bedroom
    14'-6 × 18'-4
H Bedroom
    15'-1 × 18'-4
Ceiling height
    is 12'-9"
        E. Allison del.

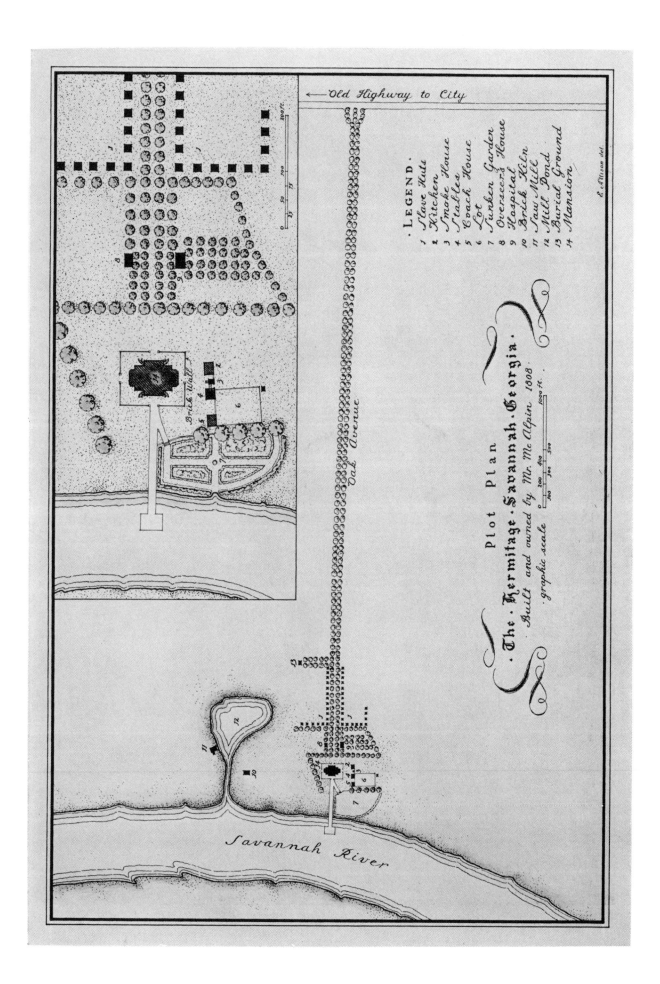

← Old Highway to City

LEGEND.
1. Slave Huts
2. Kitchen
3. Smoke House
4. Stables
5. Coach House
6. Lot
7. Sunken Garden
8. Overseer's House
9. Hospital
10. Brick Kiln
11. Saw Mill
12. Mill Pond
13. Burial Ground
14. Mansion

E. E. Allison del.

Plot Plan
.The . Hermitage . Savannah . Georgia .
Built and owned by Mr. Mc Alpin 1808.
graphic scale
0 100 200 300 400 500   1000 ft.

Oak Avenue

Brick Wall

Savannah River

23

Courtesy B. Westermann Co., Inc.   Photograph by E. Hoppe

DRAYTON HALL ON THE ASHLEY RIVER, SOUTH CAROLINA,
ENTRANCE FAÇADE

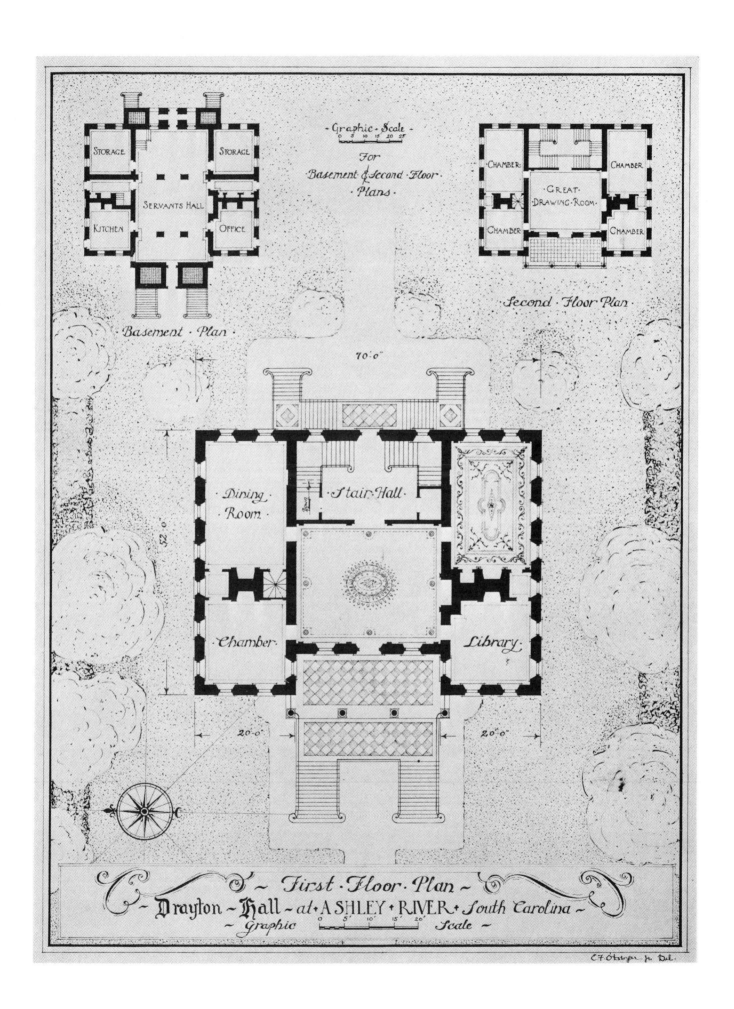

Graphic Scale
0 5 10 15 20 25

For
Basement & Second Floor
Plans

STORAGE STORAGE

SERVANTS HALL

KITCHEN OFFICE

Basement Plan

CHAMBER CHAMBER

GREAT
DRAWING ROOM

CHAMBER CHAMBER

Second Floor Plan

70'0"

Dining Room

Stair Hall

52'0"

Chamber

Library

20'0" 20'0"

~ First Floor Plan ~
~ Drayton Hall at ASHLEY RIVER South Carolina ~
~ Graphic Scale ~

0 5 10 15 20

C F Otzinger Jr Del.

Drayton Hall ~ on the ~ Ashley River ~ South Carolina

graphic scale ⅛:1:0' actual scale

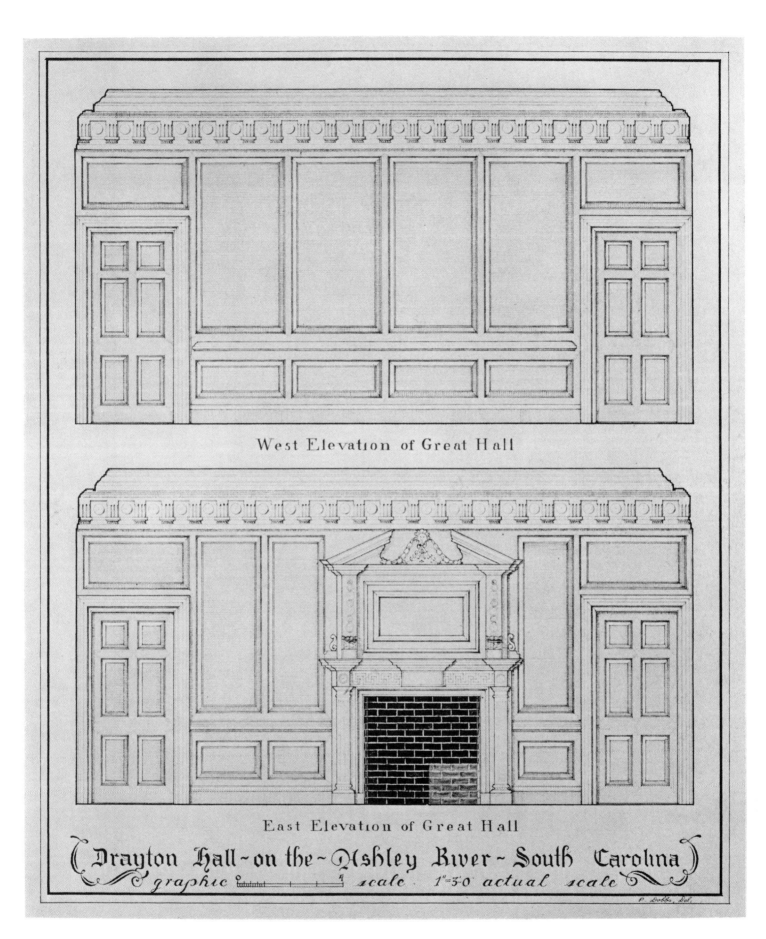

West Elevation of Great Hall

East Elevation of Great Hall

Drayton Hall ~ on the ~ Ashley River ~ South Carolina
graphic scale. 1"=3'0 actual scale

P. Dobbs. del.

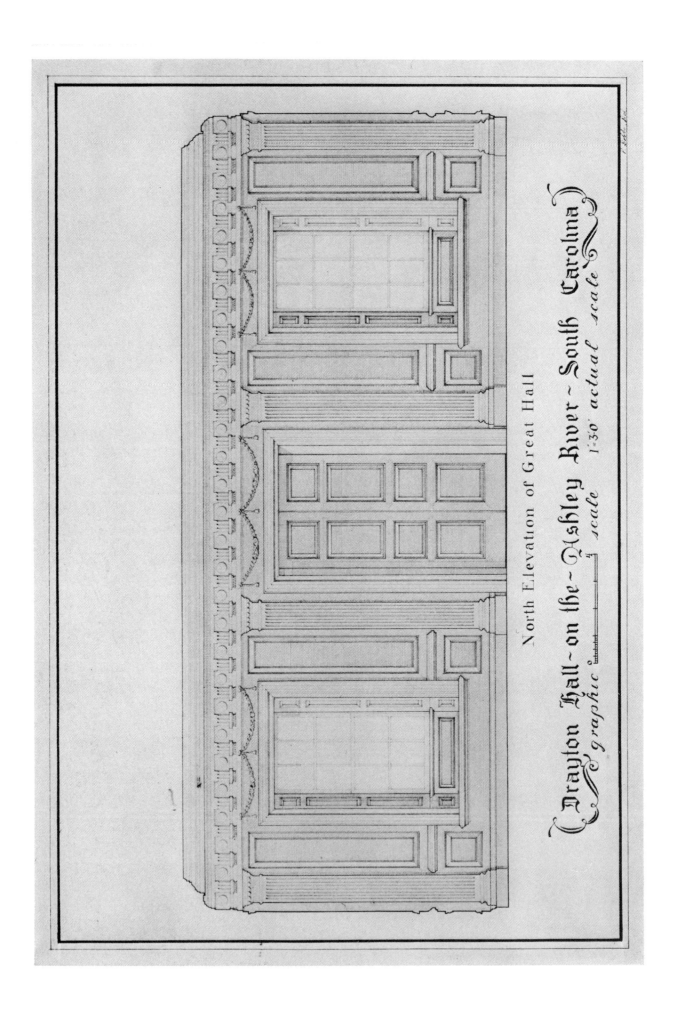

North Elevation of Great Hall

Drayton Hall ~ on the ~ Ashley River ~ South Carolina
graphic scale   ¼ scale   1″-30′ actual scale

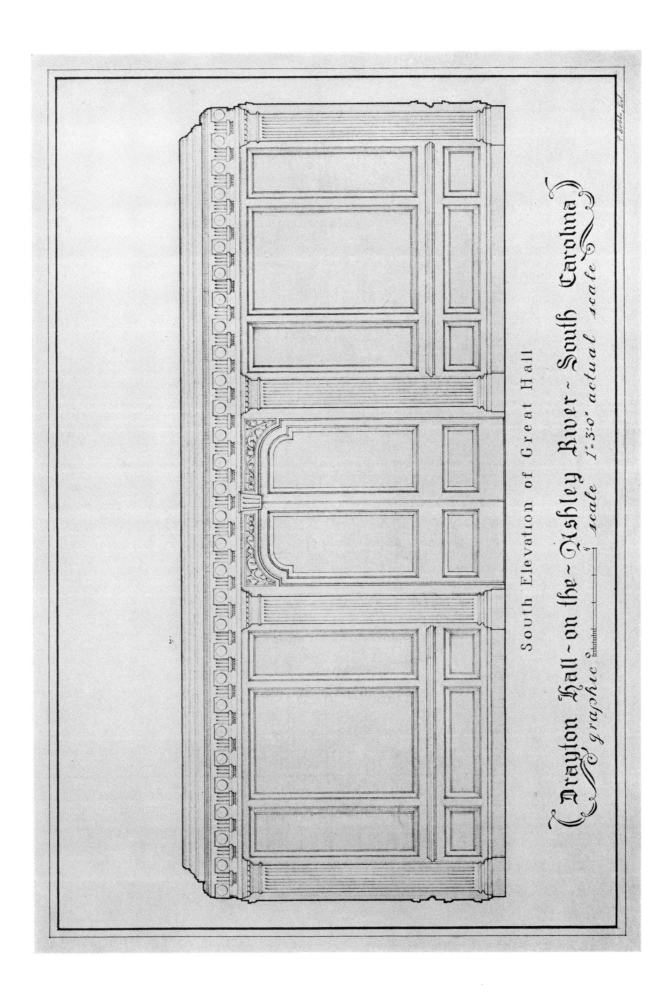

South Elevation of Great Hall

Drayton Hall ~ on the ~ Ashley River ~ South Carolina
scale 1'=3'-0" actual scale
graphic

29

THE JOSEPH MANIGAULT HOUSE, MEETING AND JOHN STREETS,
CHARLESTON, SOUTH CAROLINA, SIDE ELEVATION

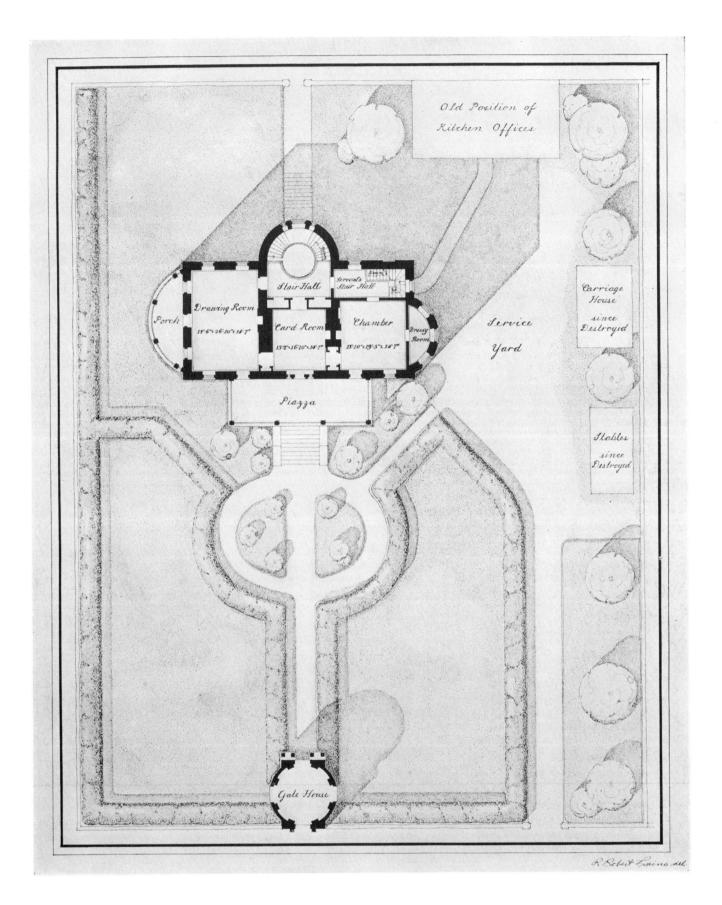

Old Position of
Kitchen Offices

Stair Hall

Servant's Stair Hall

Drawing Room
18'6"x26'10"x14'7"

Card Room
13'2"x16'10"x14'7"

Chamber
18'10"x19'5"x14'7"

Porch

Dressy Room

Service Yard

Piazza

Carriage House since Destroyed

Stables since Destroyed

Gate House

R. Robert Laino del.

The GARDEN And

SECOND FLOOR PLAN

Restored Of

The Joseph Manigault House

Meeting and John Streets CHARLESTON *South Carolina*

Graphic   0   4   8   12   16   20   *Scale*

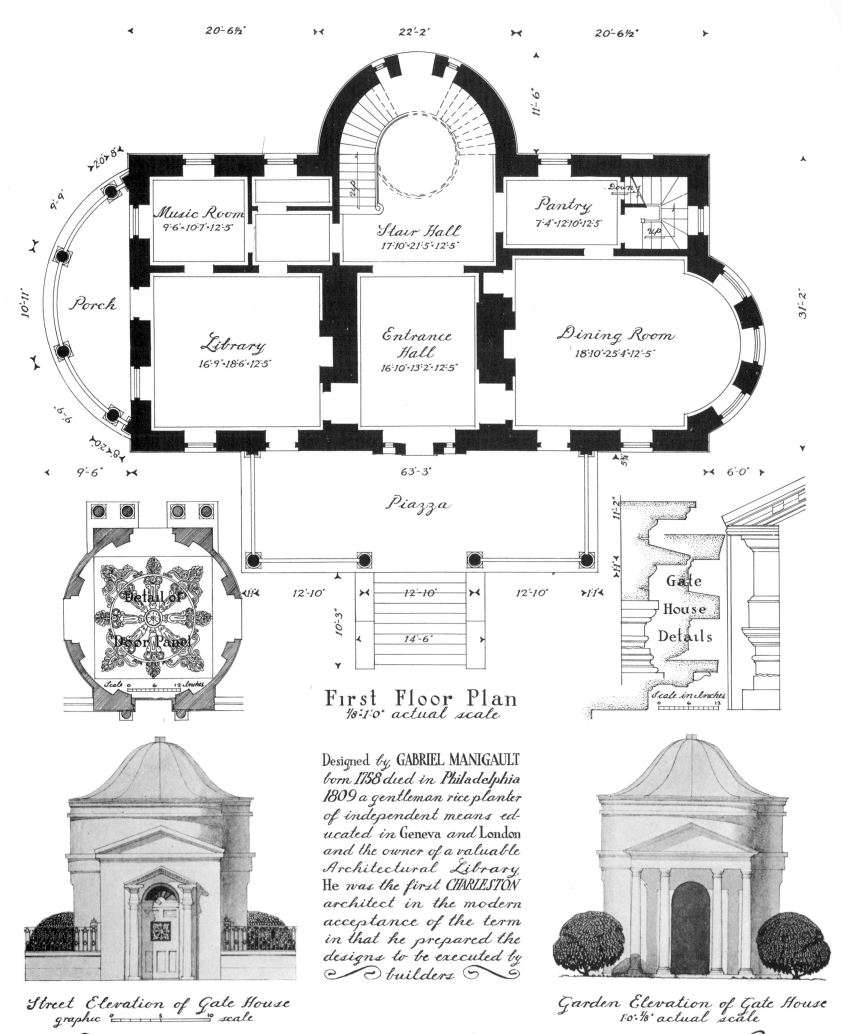

20'-6½" 22'-2" 20'-6½"

11'-6"

20'-8"

9'-9"

Music Room
9'-6"×10'-7"×12'-5"

Stair Hall
17'-10"×21'-5"×12'-5"

Pantry
7'-4"×12'-10"×12'-5"

Down

Up

10'-11"

Porch

Library
16'-9"×18'-6"×12'-5"

Entrance
Hall
16'-10"×13'-2"×12'-5"

Dining Room
18'-10"×25'-4"×12'-5"

31'-2"

6'-6"

8'-2½"

9'-6"

63'-3"

5¾"

Piazza

Detail of
Door Panel

Scale 0   6   12 Inches

12'-10"

12'-10" 12'-10"

14'-6"

10'-3"

11'-2"

11'-1"

Gate
House
Details

Scale in Inches
0   6   12

6'-0"

First Floor Plan
⅛"=1'-0" actual scale

Designed by GABRIEL MANIGAULT
born 1758 died in Philadelphia
1809 a gentleman rice planter
of independent means ed-
ucated in Geneva and London
and the owner of a valuable
Architectural Library,
He was the first CHARLESTON
architect in the modern
acceptance of the term
in that he prepared the
designs to be executed by
builders

Street Elevation of Gate House
graphic ⊢————5————⊣ scale

Garden Elevation of Gate House
1'-0":⅛" actual scale

The ~ Joseph Manigault House ~ Charleston ~ South ~ Carolina
Meeting and John Streets ~ Built about 1790

32

R. Robert Lairo del.

FRONT ELEVATION
Scale 1/16"·1'·0"

EXTERIOR
DETAILS

Porch Cornice
and Column
Scale 3/4"·1'·0"

Piazza Railing
Scale 1"·1'·0"

Entrance Door
Cornice & Pilaster
Scale 3/4"·1'·0"

John Poscott Del.

The ~Joseph Manigault House~ Charleston~ South ~ Carolina
Meeting and John Streets ~ Built about 1790

DRAWING OF THE MILES BREWTON HOUSE,
CHARLESTON, SOUTH CAROLINA, BY SCHELL LEWIS

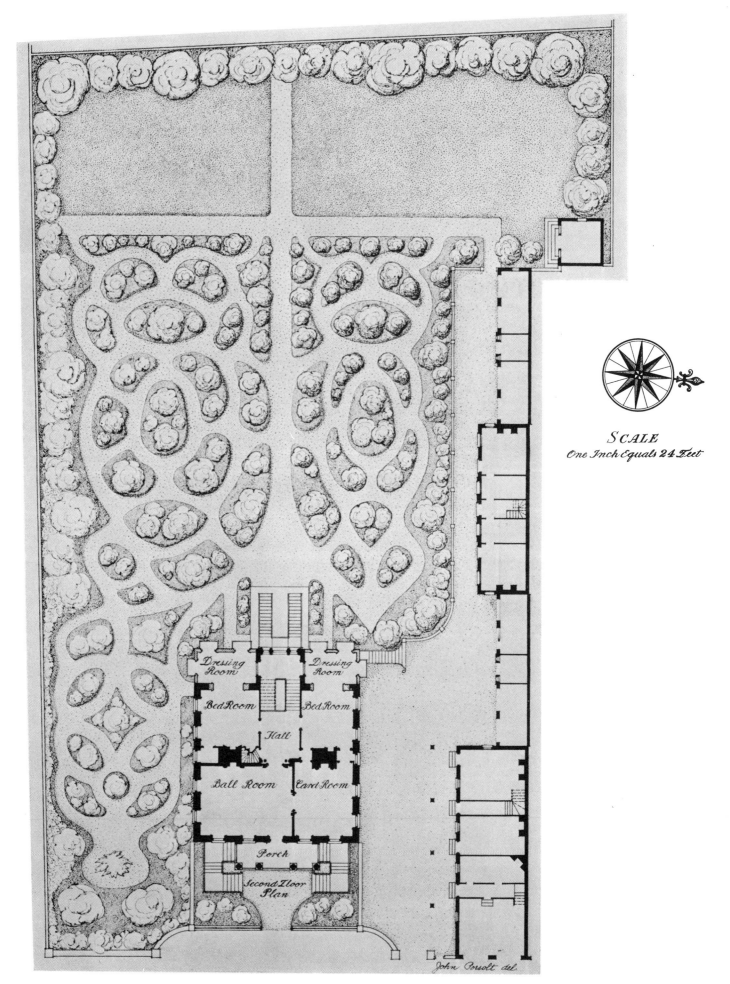

SCALE
One Inch Equals 24 Feet

Dressing Room

Dressing Room

Bed Room

Bed Room

Hall

Ball Room

Card Room

Porch

Second Floor Plan

John Corsolt del.

The Garden Plan of
The Miles Brewton House
27 King Street CHARLESTON South Carolina

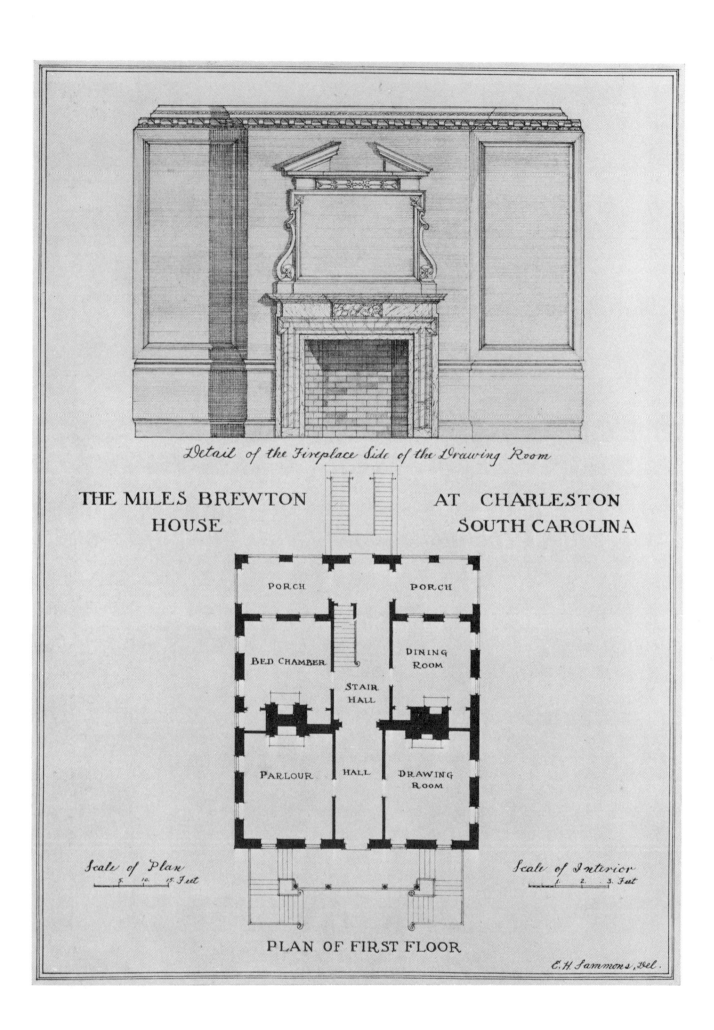

Detail of the Fireplace Side of the Drawing Room

THE MILES BREWTON
HOUSE

AT CHARLESTON
SOUTH CAROLINA

PORCH   PORCH

BED CHAMBER   DINING ROOM

STAIR HALL

PARLOUR   HALL   DRAWING ROOM

Scale of Plan
5   10   15 Feet

Scale of Interior
1   2   3 Feet

PLAN OF FIRST FLOOR

C. H. Sammons, Del.

The MILES BREWTON HOUSE
at CHARLESTON SOUTH CAROLINA
built circa 1765 by EZRA WAITE, civil
Architect and Builder from LONDON ~

Elevation DRAWN TO SCALE OF 1/16" = 1'   Details DRAWN TO SCALE OF 9/16" = 1'

PLAN OF LANTERN RING

D. COPELAND DEL.

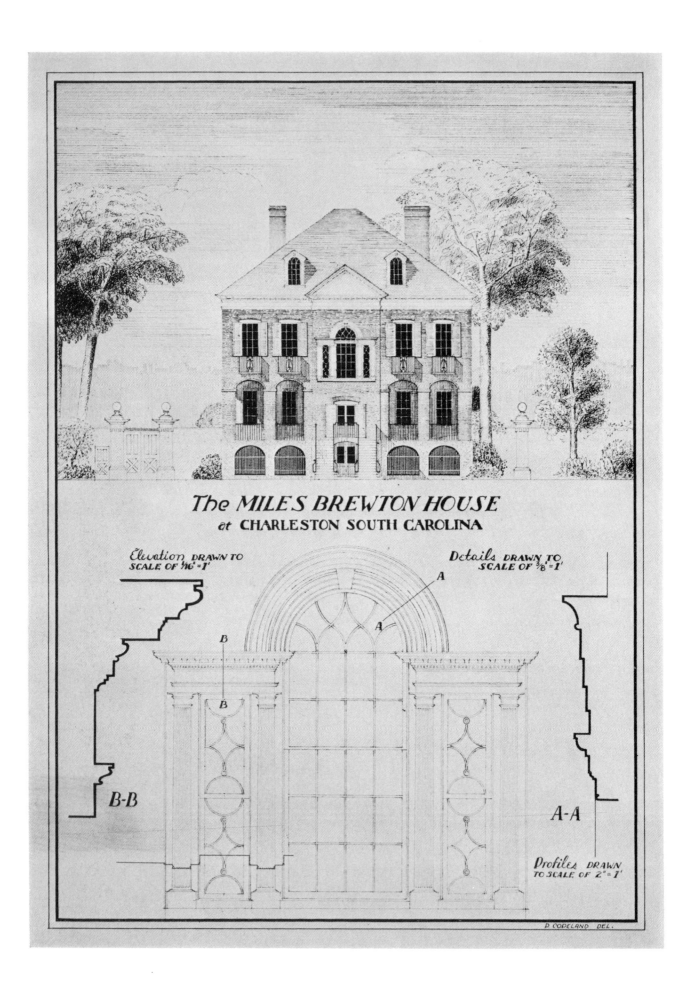

The MILES BREWTON HOUSE
at CHARLESTON SOUTH CAROLINA

Elevation DRAWN TO SCALE OF 1/16" = 1'

Details DRAWN TO SCALE OF 3/8" = 1'

A

A

B

B

B-B

A-A

Profiles DRAWN TO SCALE OF 2" = 1'

D. COPELAND DEL.

THE WILLIAM GIBBES HOUSE, CHARLESTON, SOUTH CAROLINA, ENTRANCE FAÇADE

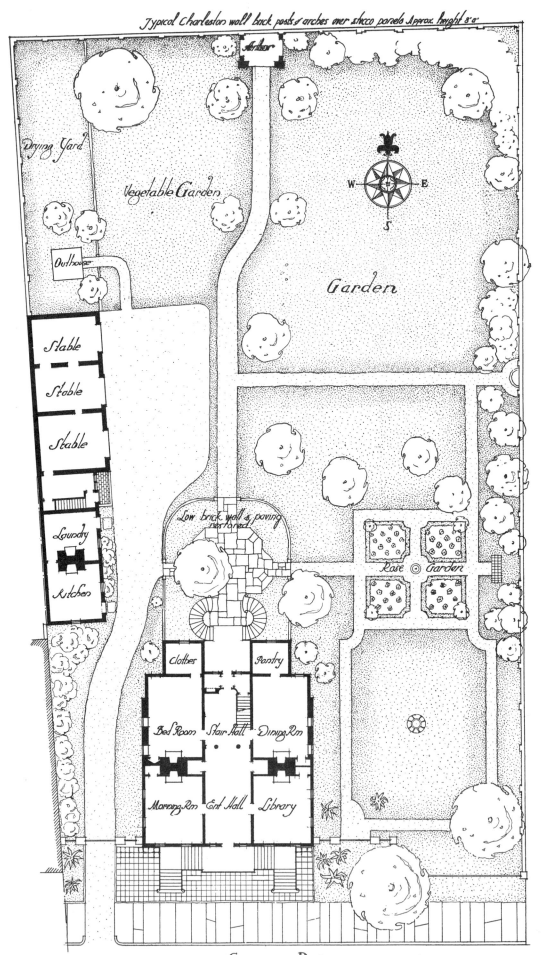

Typical Charleston wall brick posts & arches over stucco panels Approx. height 8'0"

Arbor

Drying Yard

Vegetable Garden

W E
S

Outhouse

Garden

Stable

Stable

Stable

Low brick wall & paving restored

Rose Garden

Laundry

Kitchen

Clothes   Pantry

Bed Room   Stair Hall   Dining Rm

Morning Rm   Ent Hall   Library

GARDEN PLAN

CIRCA - 1775
RESTORED 1930

The WILLIAM GIBBES Residence
Charleston South Carolina

0 5 10 20 30
graphic scale

The Garden Elevation

The WILLIAM GIBBES *Residence*
Charleston, South Carolina
Rear stairway and wings added during restoration, over existing foundation

CIRCA 1775   graphic   Scale   RESTORED 1930

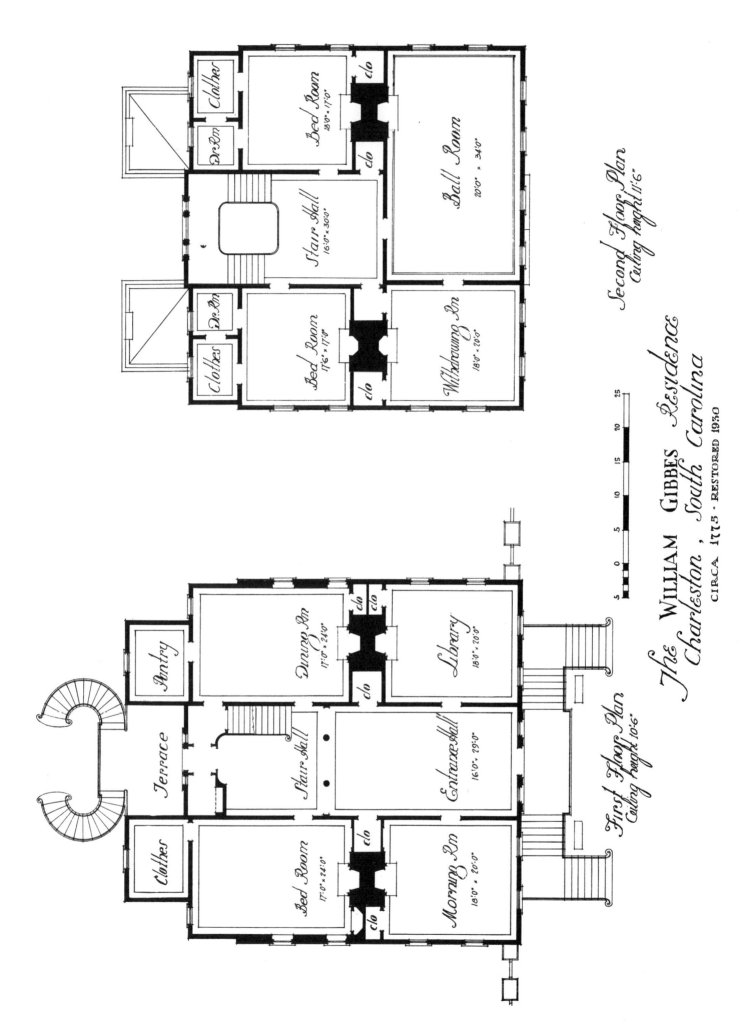

Clothes

Dr. Rm.

Bed Room
18'0" × 17'0"

clo

clo

Stair Hall
16'0" × 30'0"

Ball Room
20'0" × 34'0"

Clothes

Dr. Rm.

Bed Room
17'6" × 17'0"

clo

Withdrawing Rm
18'0" × 20'0"

Second Floor Plan
Ceiling height 11'6"

25

20

15

10

5

0

5

Pantry

Dining Rm
17'0" × 24'0"

clo
clo

clo

Library
18'0" × 20'0"

Terrace

Stair Hall

Entrance Hall
16'0" × 29'0"

Clothes

Bed Room
17'0" × 24'0"

clo

clo

Morning Rm
18'0" × 20'0"

First Floor Plan
Ceiling height 10'6"

The WILLIAM GIBBES Residence
Charleston, South Carolina
CIRCA 1775 · RESTORED 1930

42

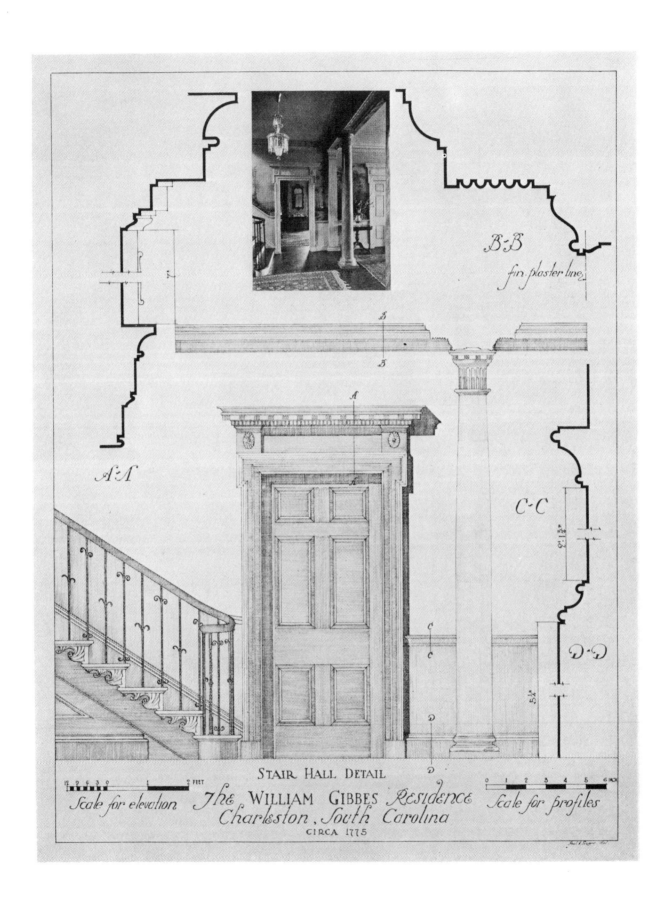

B·B

fin. plaster line

A·A

C·C

2'·1 3"

G·G

5"

STAIR HALL DETAIL

Scale for elevation *The* WILLIAM GIBBES *Residence* Scale for profiles
Charleston, South Carolina
CIRCA 1775

E·E

C C

Reflected plan

D·D

Rosette

B·B

A·A

NORTH WALL · WITHDRAWING ROOM
Second Floor

Plan at upper pilaster

Plan at lower pilaster

Scale for profiles

3 INCH 4 3 2 1 0

Scale for details

0 4 8 12 16 20 INCH

12 9 6 3 0 1 2 3 FEET

The WILLIAM GIBBES Residence
Charleston, South Carolina
CIRCA 1775

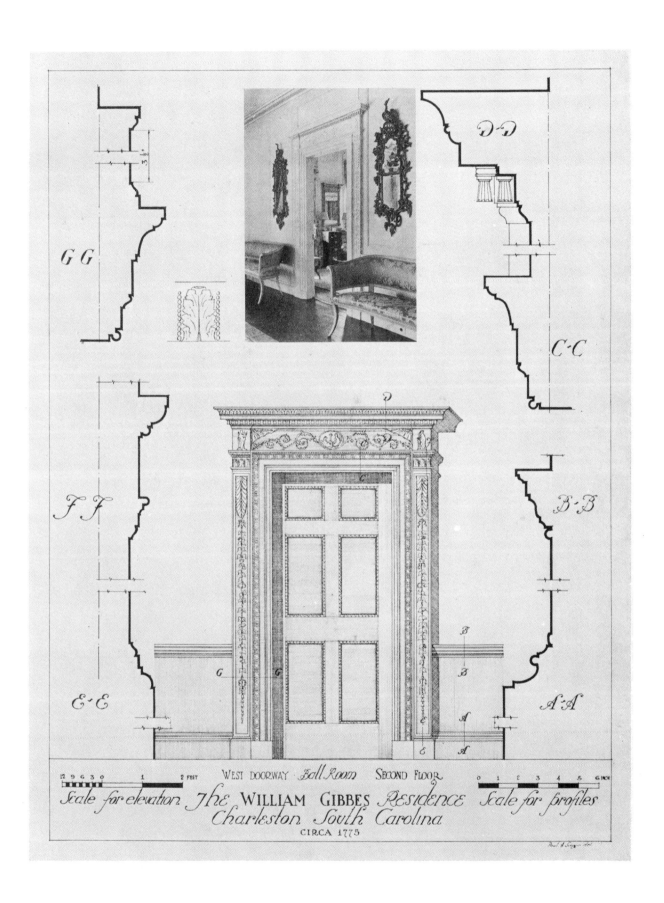

GG

GG

3½"

CC

FF

BB

D

B

B

G

G

C

E

A

A

EE

AA

West Doorway *Ball Room* Second Floor

12 9 6 3 0   1   2 Feet

0 1 2 3 4 5 6 Inch

Scale for elevation The WILLIAM GIBBES *Residence* *Scale for profiles*
Charleston South Carolina
CIRCA 1775

45

STRATFORD, WESTMORELAND COUNTY, VIRGINIA, GARDEN FAÇADE

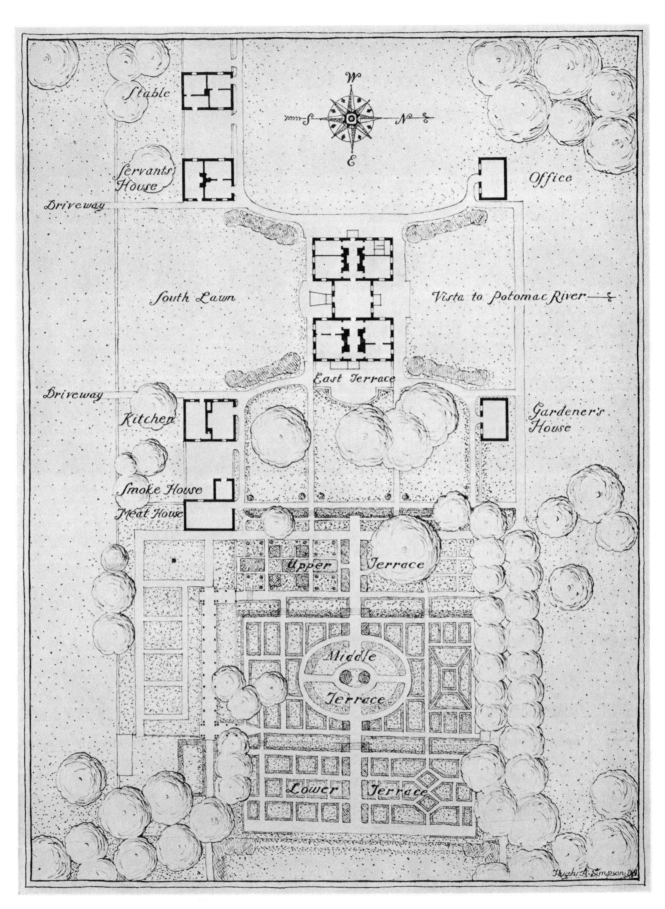

Stable

Servants House

Driveway

Office

South Lawn

Vista to Potomac River

Driveway

East Terrace

Kitchen

Gardener's House

Smoke House

Meat House

Upper Terrace

Middle Terrace

Lower Terrace

Hugh A. Simpson

The Garden and Dependencies of
Stratford ~ Westmoreland County ~ Virginia
Restoration plan by Morley J. Williams ~ Graphic scale 20 40 60

The South or D...
Stratford—Westmor...
BUILT BY Colonel...
Graphic Scal...

way Facade of
d County ~ Virginia·

omas Lee IN 1730

5 FT.   10 FT.   15 FT.   20

Hugh A. Simpson Del.

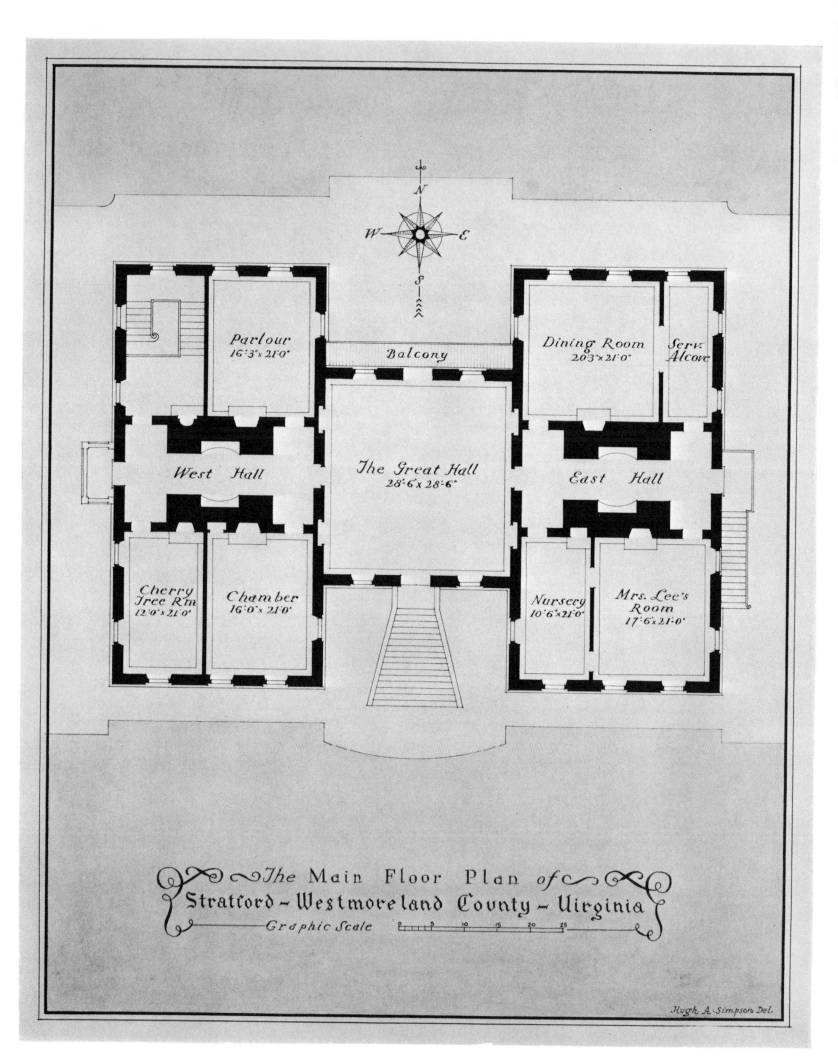

N

W E

S

Parlour
16'·3"x 21'·0"

Balcony

Dining Room
20'·3"x 21'·0"

Serv.
Alcove

West Hall

The Great Hall
28'·6"x 28'·6"

East Hall

Cherry
Tree Rm
12'·0"x 21'·0"

Chamber
16'·0"x 21'·0"

Nursery
10'·6"x 21'·0"

Mrs. Lee's
Room
17'·6"x 21'·0"

The Main Floor Plan of
Stratford - Westmoreland County - Virginia
Graphic Scale

Hugh A. Simpson Del.

50

The South Wall of the Great Hall

Stratford · Westmoreland County · Virginia ·

Executed in heart pine and painted. ~ The north wall is identical to the south wall.

Graphic 0   5   10 Scale
            feet.

Hugh A. Simpson. del.

ENTRANCE FAÇADE OF MOUNT AIRY, RICHMOND COUNTY, VIRGINIA

The house has remained in the possession of the Tayloe family since it was built
by Colonel John Tayloe in 1758

VIEW TO
RAPPAHANNOCK RIVER

TOOL HOUSE

TOOL HOUSE

FIR TREES

SUNKEN GARDEN

BOWLING GREEN

ARBOR

ARBOR

STEPS

ORANGERIE

SMOKE HOUSE

DAIRY

COUNTING HOUSE

OFFICE

Scale in feet

The Garden Plan of
Mount Airy Richmond County Virginia
RESTORED SHOWING
THE RESIDENCE *with dependent* WINGS *forecourt out buildings paths
drives parterres* ORANGERIE *garden pavilions steps &* TERRACES

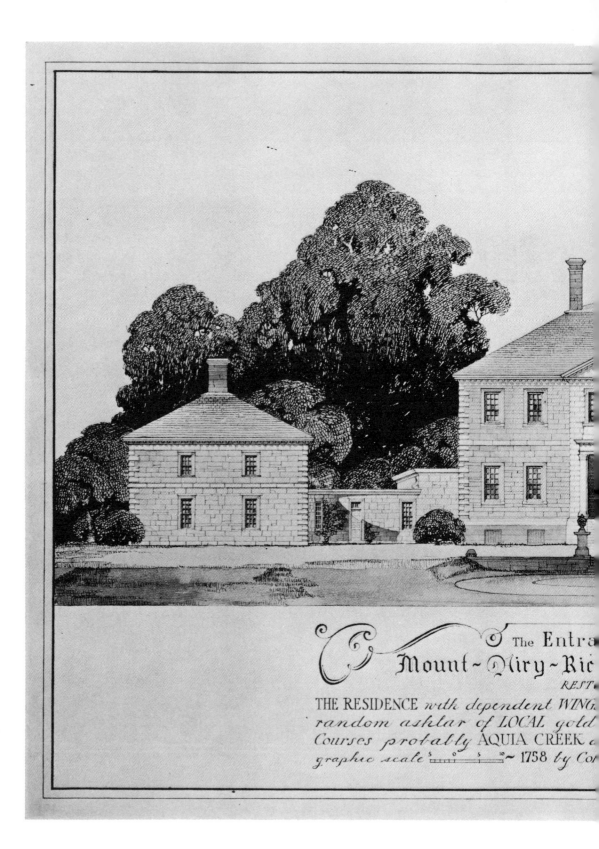

The Entra
Mount~Airy~Ric
REST
THE RESIDENCE *with dependent WING*
random ashlar of LOCAL gold
Courses probably AQUIA CREEK
graphic scale ~ 1758 *by Co*

cade of
~ County ~ Virginia
WING
recourt WALL surfaces are of
stone Quoins Columns and String
LISH PORTLAND stone built in
N TAYLOE ~ 1/16"=1'-0" actual scale

Mitchell Wooten Del.

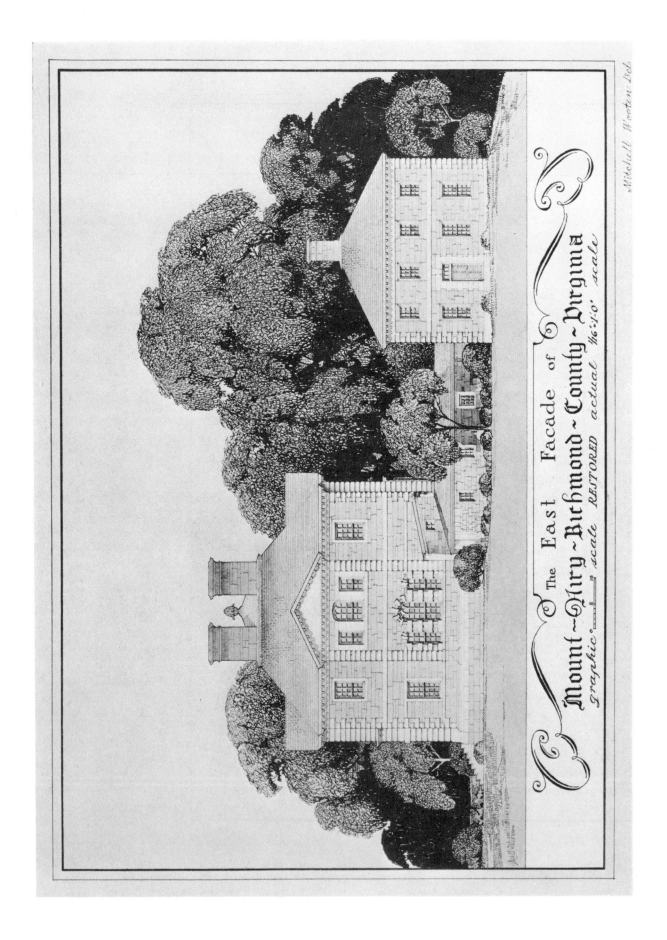

The East Facade of
Mount ~ Airy ~ Richmond ~ County ~ Virginia
Graphic's ⌐───┐ ⌐───┐ scale   RESTORED   actual ¼"=1'-0" scale

Mitchell Wooten del.

Mitchell Wooten Del.

Detail of South Facade of
Mount~Airy~Richmond~County~Virginia
Drawn to *Scale of ½"=1'-0"*

57

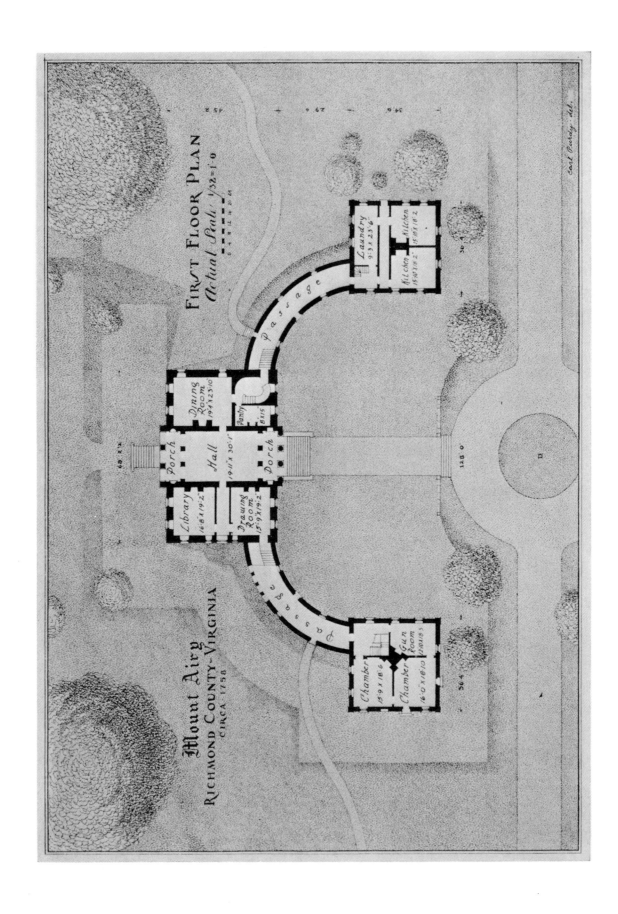

Mount Airy
RICHMOND COUNTY·VIRGINIA
CIRCA 1758

FIRST FLOOR PLAN
Actual Scale ⅛₂=1'-0

58

THE GARDEN FAÇADE OF MOUNT AIRY, RICHMOND COUNTY, VIRGINIA

ENTRANCE FAÇADE OF WESTOVER, CHARLES CITY COUNTY, VIRGINIA

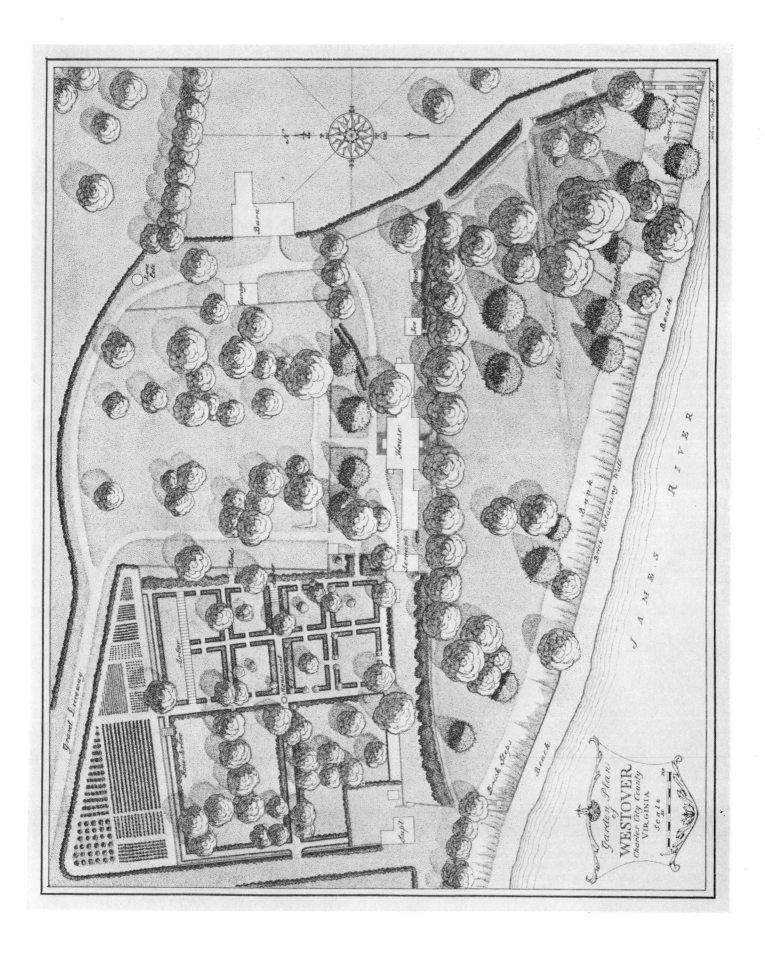

Garden Plan
of
WESTOVER
Charles City County
VIRGINIA
Scale

JAMES RIVER

W
Charles E

N

actual scale of house 1/16":1'0"

The Clairvoyée is the only existing example in Virginia. Entrance to the enclosure is gained through a gateway enriched by an elaborate wrot iron overthrow in the scroll work of which appears the cypher of the builder

WILLIAM BYRD II born March 28, 167 house. The façade is probably building in America. Both fr the doorways, which are in ea steps, of pyramidal form. The of brick painted white. The color

ER ☙

Virginia

ade

15

uilder of the present Westover
n than that of any Georgian
actically identical except for
ached by extremely wide stone
ring course of the main house are
nections, built later, are omitted.

D

A series of carved stone finials on
stucco covered piers are varied and
interesting and were without a doubt
carved in England. The material appears
to be Portland stone as are the steps &
stone doors of both fronts of the house
Detail ½"=1'0" scale

B

The First Floor Plan of
WESTOVER
Charles City County, Virginia
Circa 1726
scale 3/64"=1'·0"

Mitchell Wooton Del.

Gate House

Kitchen

Office

Living Room
18'·7" x 24'·5"

Hall

Dining Room
18' x 36'·9"

Parlour
16'·3" x 24'·5"

64

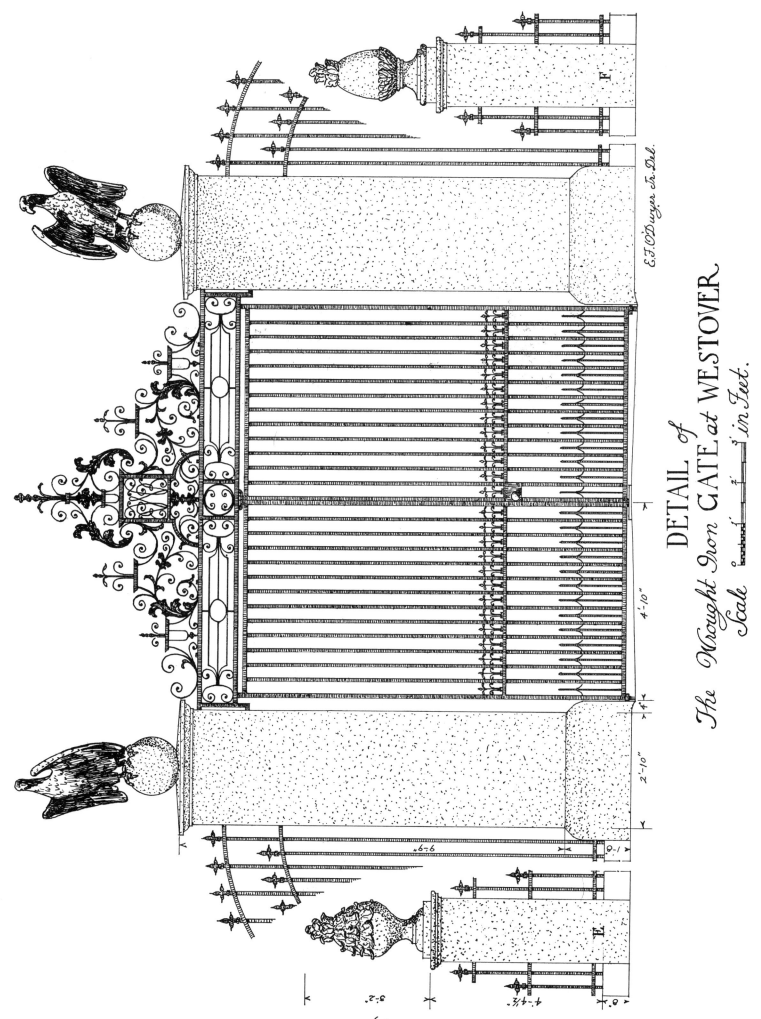

DETAIL of
The Wrought Iron GATE at WESTOVER.
Scale ⊢┴┴┴┴┤━━━━┥ ⅓ in Feet.

E.J.O'Dwyer Fr. Del.

65

WESTOVER
Charles City County
Verginia.

The Main GATEWAY and the smaller Garden Gates are among the very finest examples of English Wrought Iron in America. The simplicity of the Gates together with the elaborate Scroll-work of the Overthrow, and the flanking Bird forms lend much in dignity and charm to the Approach. In the Scroll-work of the Overthrow appears the Cypher of the Builder WILLIAM BYRD II The flanking Bays of the Clairvoyée were probably intended to be filled with Wrought Iron, but whether this scheme was ever fulfilled is not known. Until recently however a heavy Picket Fence of wood served the purpose. The Modern Cast Iron Fence has been recently substituted.

GARDEN FAÇADE OF MONTICELLO NEAR CHARLOTTESVILLE, VIRGINIA

The Lawn

Garden Portico

Drawing
Room
24'0" × 28'6"

Study
11'6" × 18'0"

To Body Servants
Room Above

Jefferson's
Bed
Room
13'10" × 18'0"

Bed
Alcove

Dining
Room
19'0" × 18'0"

Promenade
(UNDERGROUND
PASSAGE BELOW)

Piazza
13'0" × 20'0"

TOILET CL.

Passage
UP   DOWN

BALCONY ABOVE

ALCOVE

Passage
DOWN   UP

Piazza
13'0" × 20'0"

Promenade
(UNDERGROUND
PASSAGE BELOW)

The
Hall
24'0" × 32'0"

Library
14'6" × 19'0"

Sitting
Room
14'8" × 19'0"

Bed
Room
14'8" × 19'0"

Madison's
Bed
Room
14'6" × 19'0"

Entrance
Portico

Grass

Grass

Brick Walk

★ ★ MONTICELLO ★ ★
· NEAR ·
· CHARLOTTESVILLE ~ VIRGINIA ·

Designed and built by Thomas Jefferson during
the years 1771 to 1775 ~ Jefferson began the remodelling of the south facade of Monticello in 1796, which
was completed in 1806

Graphic   2'   10'   20'   30'   Scale

Wallace Heath del.

68

ENTRANCE HALL OF MONTICELLO NEAR CHARLOTTESVILLE, VIRGINIA

It is probable the balcony was added when Jefferson decided to put in two mezzanine floors, adding the stairways at the same time

MOUNT VERNON

THE *present MOUNT VERNON dwelling had its beginning in 1743, when Major LAWRENCE WASH-INGTON built a small cottage on the land inherited from his father. MOUNT VERNON was named in honour of Admiral VERNON of the British Navy, under whom LAWRENCE WASHINGTON served in a West Indian campaign. The latter died in 1752 and left the estate to his infant daughter, SARAH, who survived her father by only a few months. On her death the property went to GEORGE WASH-INGTON with certain provisions as to the widow's rights in the income derived from the estate.*

In 1758 he became engaged to the widow MAR-THA CUSTIS and realized that the present cottage was inadequate for her use. Rapidly plan-ned and executed, the eight-room house was thoroughly overhauled, reroofed, resheathed, its foundation walls of brick reconstructed, rooms papered or painted, and two small detached wings added, open arcades at each end connecting them to the cottage.

They were married in January 6, 1759 and it was not until spring was well advanced that the couple set forth for MOUNT VERNON. On ac-count of their wide popularity and the increas-ing number of guests to be entertained greater ex-pansion of their dwelling became imperative. The chief essential was a more spacious room for seat-ing the company at meals; for this WASHINGTON planned, at the north end, an extension suitable for ban-quet hall or reception. At the opposite end he con-trived a library and butler's pantry, on the first floor, and a commodious bedroom for himself and wife just above. The scheme also embraced important adjacent buildings, such as kitchen, office, wash-house, smoke-house, etc. as shown on garden plan. In 1773

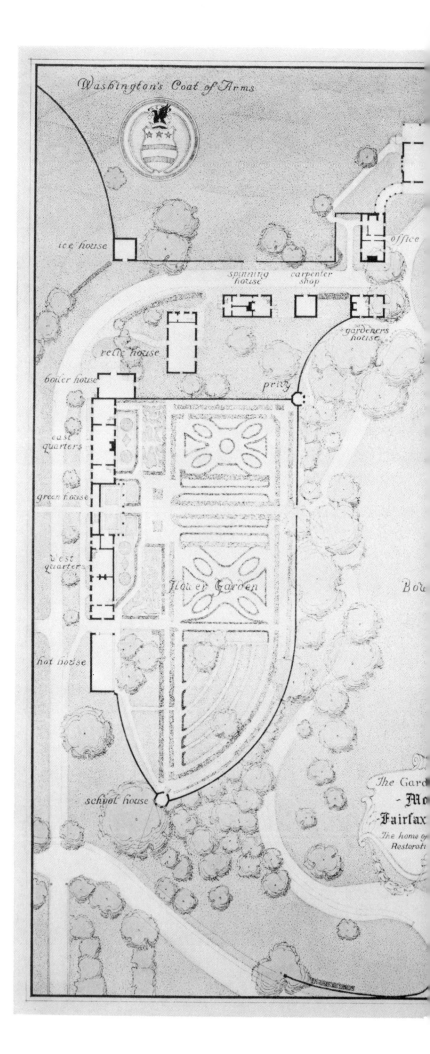

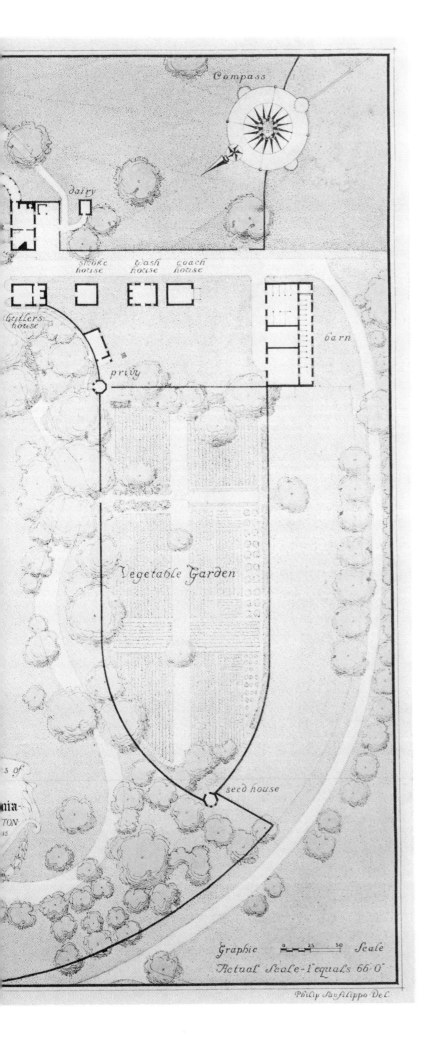

he removed the cottage wings, built the new family kitchen, and had made fair progress with the south-end extension of his dwelling when called away, in 1775 to attend the Continental Congress, where he was unanimously chosen as Commander-in-Chief of the Army. He did not see his home again until 1781, on his hurried trip to Yorktown. WASHINGTON died on the night of December 14TH 1799.

In 1802 Judge BUSHROD WASHING-TON inherited the mansion and 4,000 acres and found practically an empty house - which he soon adequately furnished. Attributed to him were certain changes, namely the ornamental balustrade on the East Portico, the porch at the south-end of the building and the lengthening of the windows opening on it.

The frame timbers of the buildings are of hand hewn oak, mortised and pinned. The sheathing is of long-leaf pine, beveled in such a fashion as to give the exterior the appearance of stone blocks. A wood filler, or preservative, called "Ship Varnish," was first applied, followed by paint with sand finish to give the effect of stone. The East Portico foot-square blocks of pavement are of gray and red stratified sandstone and were quarried at St. Bees Head in Cumberland, on Lord LONDALE'S estate, west coast of England.

Great thanks is due to the MOUNT VERNON Ladies' Association for the infinite care with which the house has been restored and for providing the funds with which it is being maintained

Owing to the memorial character of MOUNT VERNON it is the wish of the MOUNT VERNON Ladies' Association that it should never be reproduced in whole or in part.

DRAWING OF THE ENTRANCE FAÇADE OF MT. VERNON, FAIRFAX COUNTY, VIRGINIA, BY CHESTER B. PRICE

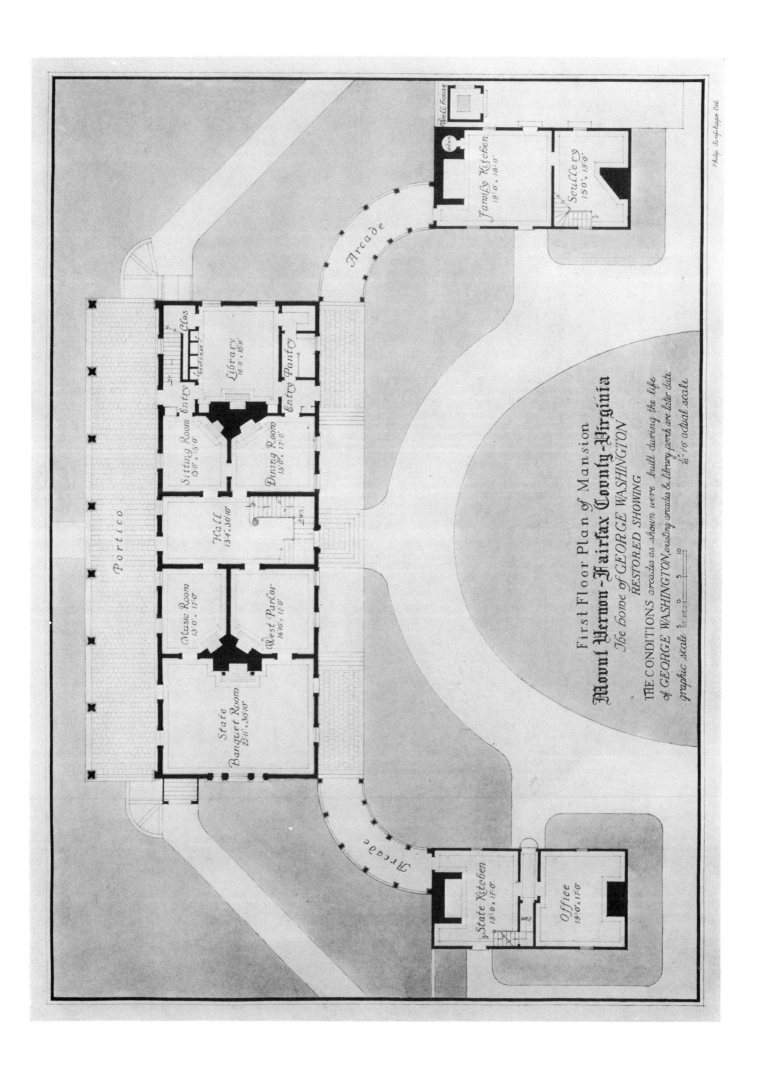

First Floor Plan of Mansion
Mount Vernon ~ Fairfax County ~ Virginia
The home of GEORGE WASHINGTON
RESTORED SHOWING

THE CONDITIONS *arcades as shown were built during the life
of GEORGE WASHINGTON, existing arcades & library porch are fair data
$\frac{1}{16}$:1:0 actual scale*

graphic scale

Philip Scröbtapper Del.

Portico

State Banquet Room 22'11'×30'10'

Music Room 13'0'×17'0'

West Parlor 16'10'×17'0'

Hall 13'4'×30'10'

Sitting Room Entry 13'0'×15'0'

Library 16'11'×15'11'

Clos

Dining Room 13'0'×17'0'

Entry Pantry

Arcade

Well House

Family Kitchen 19'0'×18'0'

Scullery 15'0'×19'0'

State Kitchen 19'0'×17'0'

Office 19'0'×17'0'

Arcade

73

West Elevation of MOUNT VERNON home of George Washington, First President of the UNITED STATES of AMERICA. Located on the POTOMAC RIVER in VIRGINIA. Scale – 1/16" = 1'-0"

UNITED STATES OF AMERICA

The SIDING of the MAIN HOUSE is of WOOD cut in a manner to resemble RUSTICATED STONE. The WINGS are also of WOOD with rusticated QUOINS. The ARCADES are shown here according to an old drawing.

VIRGINIA
SIC SEMPER TYRANNIS

Earl Purdy & John Loughnane, dels.

MOUNT VERNON ~ North Elevation.
Scale 1/16" = 1'-0"

0 2 4 6 8 10 12 14 16

John Singleton / Earl Rouse del.

RIVER FRONT OF MOUNT VERNON, FAIRFAX COUNTY VIRGINIA

River Elevation
OF
MOUNT VERNON
HOME OF
George Washington
SCALE
1/16 INCH EQUALS 1'-0"

Carl Purdy & John Loughnane dels.

Photograph by Trowbridge

ENTRANCE HALL AND STAIRWAY OF MOUNT VERNON,
FAIRFAX COUNTY, VIRGINIA

DETAIL OF DOORWAY AND PEDIMENT LEADING FROM ENTRANCE
HALL TO THE SMALL SITTING ROOM, MOUNT VERNON,
FAIRFAX COUNTY, VIRGINIA

THE WEST PARLOUR, MOUNT VERNON, FAIRFAX COUNTY, VIRGINIA

Photograph by Trowbridge

FAMILY DINING ROOM OF MOUNT VERNON, FAIRFAX COUNTY, VIRGINIA

Banquet Hall Mount Vernon
Scale of Elevation ⊢ ⊣ ⊢ ⊣ ft   Scale of details ⊢ ⊣ ⊢ ⊣ inches

This Banquet Hall formed part of the additions which General Geo. Washington had built to the original house. This work began in the year of Our Lord 1773

The walls and ceiling are of plaster, painted. The trimmings are of wood, painted. The doors are built of mahogany. The marble mantel was sent from England.

Reflected Plan of the Ceiling

Elevation of the South Wall

Section

Chair-rail

Baseboard

Doorhead

Cornice & Ceiling Ornament

John Loughnane Del.

84

PORCH CORNICE

Mount Vernon
Exterior Details

PORCH COLUMN

Scale of details 9 inches   Scale of Palladian Window   feet   John Loughnane Del

The South or Entrance Facade of

Oatlands ~ Loudoun ~ County ~ Virginia
1/16"=1'-0" actual scale

OATLANDS was built in 1800 by GEORGE CARTER Esquire the Son of ROBERT CARTER of NOMINI HALL in VIRGINIA the PORTICO being added in 1830 ~ The CUPOLA has long since disappeared but is restored in this Drawing on the original BASE ~ The HOUSE is of BRICK covered with STUCCO painted yellow with white painted TRIM ~

Frances F. King del.

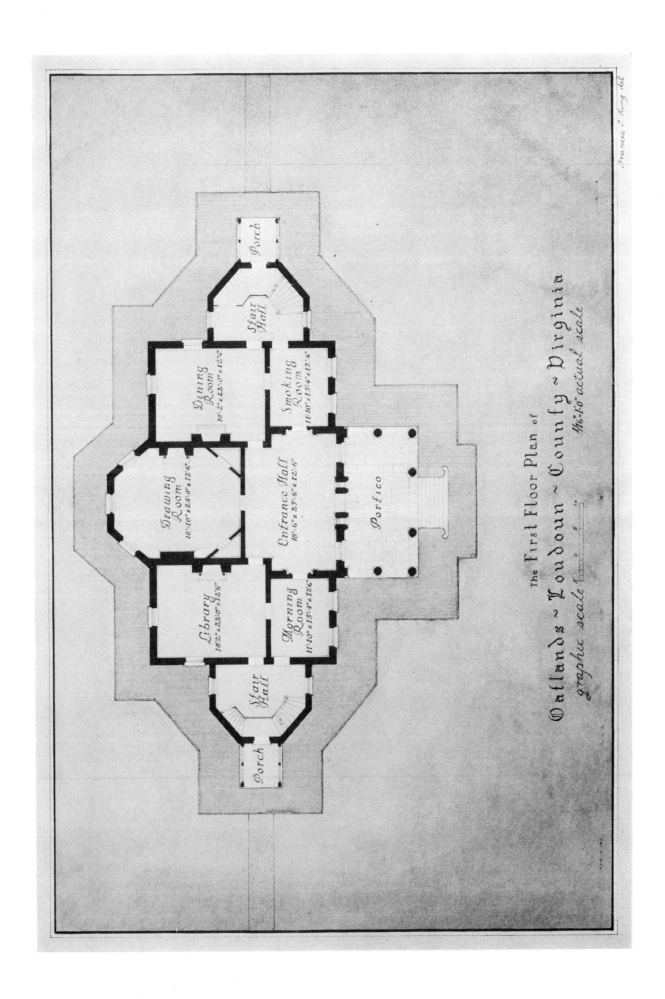

Porch

Stair Hall

Dining Room
18'-4" x 22'-0" x 12'-6"

Smoking Room
11'-10" x 15'-4" x 12'-6"

Drawing Room
18'-10" x 25'-8" x 12'-6"

Entrance Hall
18'-6" x 37'-6" x 12'-6"

Portico

Library
18'-4" x 23'-0" x 12'-6"

Morning Room
11'-10" x 15'-4" x 12'-6"

Stair Hall

Porch

The First Floor Plan of

Oatlands ~ Loudoun ~ County ~ Virginia
1/16"-1'-0" actual scale

graphic scale   5   0   5   10

Francis T. Long del

87

The Garden has been restored by Mrs William Corcoran Eustis, the present Owner. The various Terraces, Levels, Walls and Divisions are, however, in the form of the original Design

Francis T. King del

Burial Vault

Servants' Quarters

Studio

Garden House

Second Floor Plan

The Garden Plan of
Oatlands
Loudoun County
Virginia
graphic scale
actual scale 1"=60'-0"

88

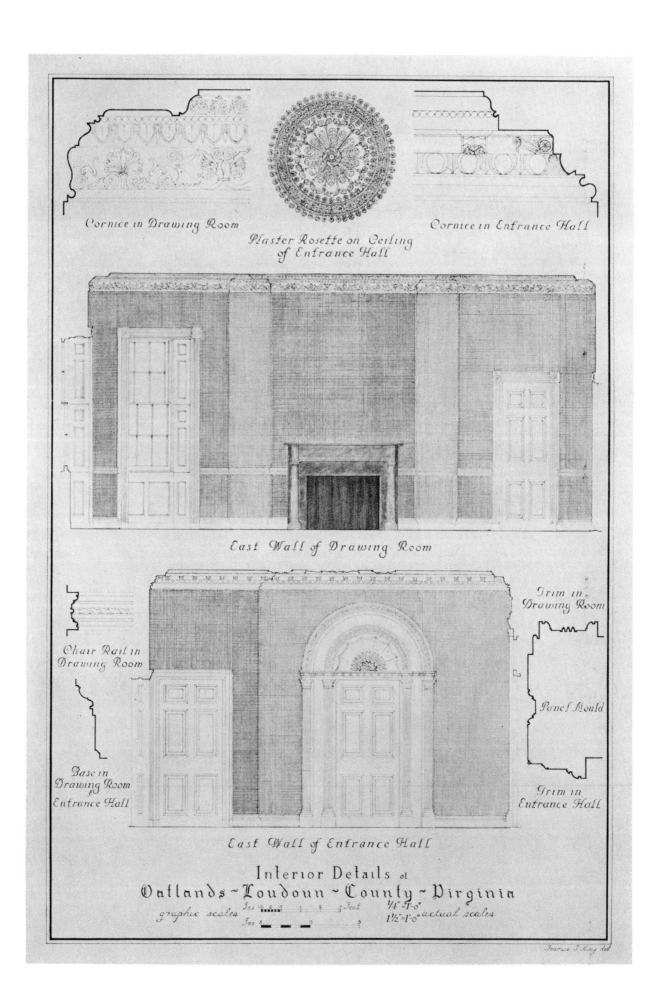

Cornice in Drawing Room

Plaster Rosette on Ceiling
of Entrance Hall

Cornice in Entrance Hall

East Wall of Drawing Room

Chair Rail in
Drawing Room

Base in
Drawing Room
&
Entrance Hall

Trim in
Drawing Room

Panel Mould

Trim in
Entrance Hall

East Wall of Entrance Hall

Interior Details of
Oatlands ~ Loudoun ~ County ~ Virginia
graphic scales   ¼"-1'-0"
1½"-1'-0" actual scales

Francis J. King del.

89

DRAWING ROOM AT OATLANDS, LOUDOUN COUNTY, VIRGINIA

GARDEN STEPS AT OATLANDS, LOUDOUN COUNTY, VIRGINIA

The North o[f]
Bremo ~ Fluvan[na]

GRAPHIC ⊢——————⊣ [F]SCALE

THE RESIDENCE *as originally designed by* **THOMAS JEFFERSON** *in 1815. The building was built for* **JOHN** *gates spanning the semi-circular ha-ha to keep the cattle off the Lawn as was done by The walls are of a smooth rather dark cherry colored brick wood cornice brick columns covered of the windows. The shutters are a black green. The blind arches of the dependent WINGS and th*

Facade of
...nty ~ Virginia
1/16:1:0" ACTUAL SCALE

...CKE Esq. the first stone being laid July 18, 1818. In the foreground is shown the bridge stile and
...t Mount Vernon. The pediment was originally surmounted by a weather vane as at Monticello
...of a warm tone matching the limestone string courses keystones and flat arch lintels and sills
...are stuccoed to match the columns. The pedimented trim of the main door is of wood.

THE ENTRANCE FAÇADE OF BREMO, FLUVANNA COUNTY, VIRGINIA

Showing the Ha-Ha with its bridge and stile. Beyond the terraces extends the broad expanse of the Valley of the James

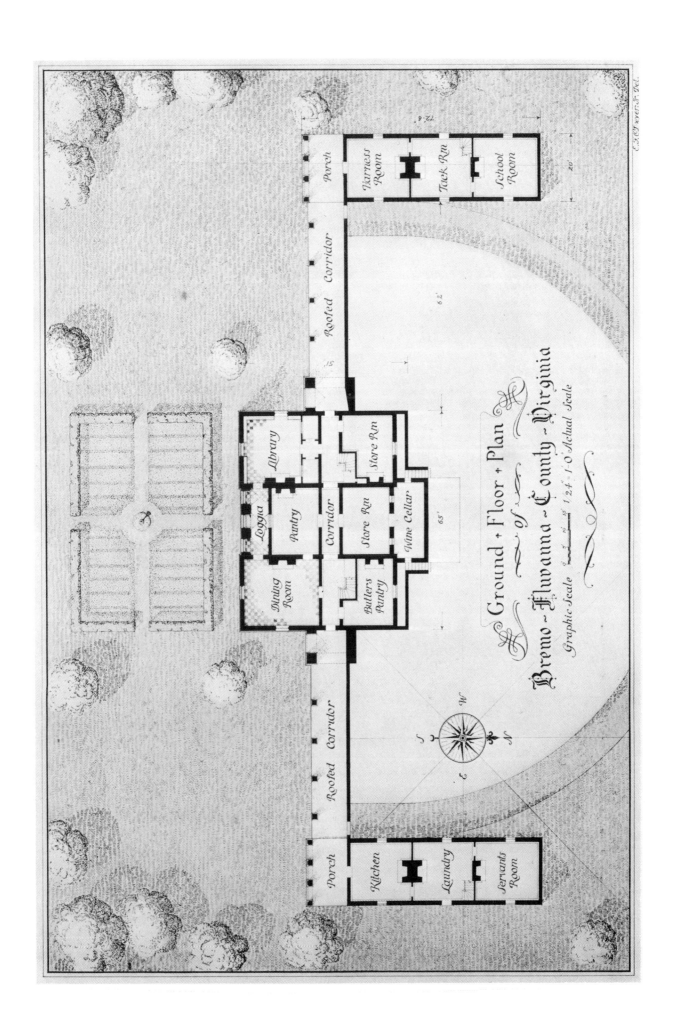

Ground + Floor + Plan
of
Bremo ~ Fluvanna ~ County ~ Virginia
Graphic Scale   1:24" - 1'-0" Actual Scale

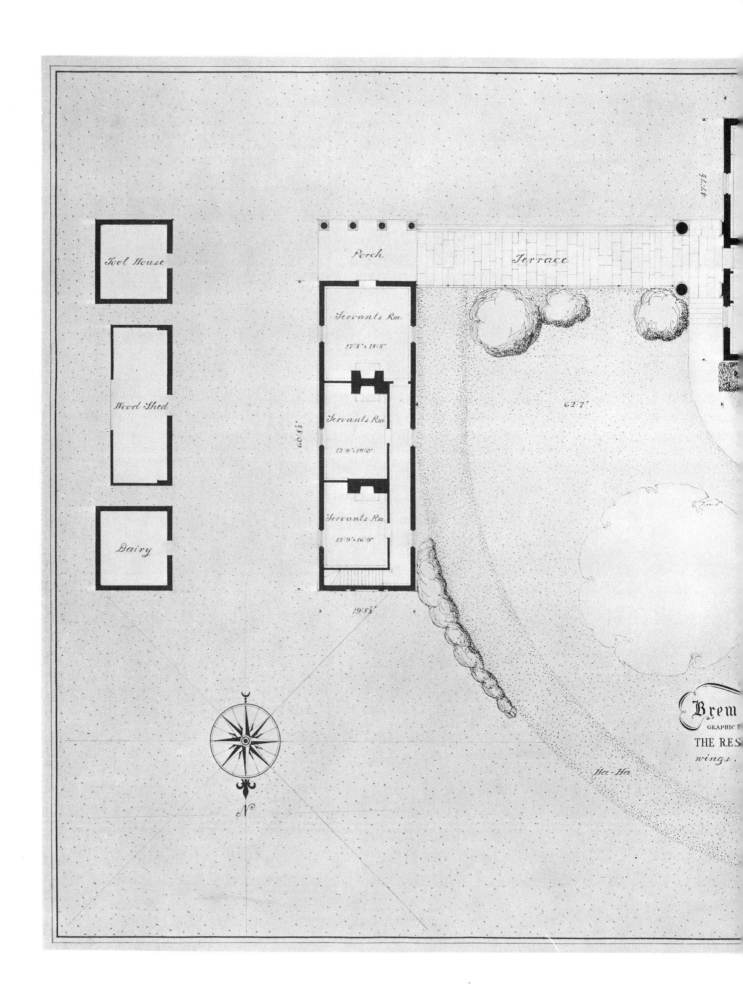

Tool House

Wood Shed

Dairy

Porch

Terrace

Servants Rm.
17'8" x 18'5"

Servants Rm.
12'9" x 19'0"

Servants Rm.
12'9" x 16'9"

62'7"

Brem

GRAPHIC

THE RES

wings

Ha-Ha

N

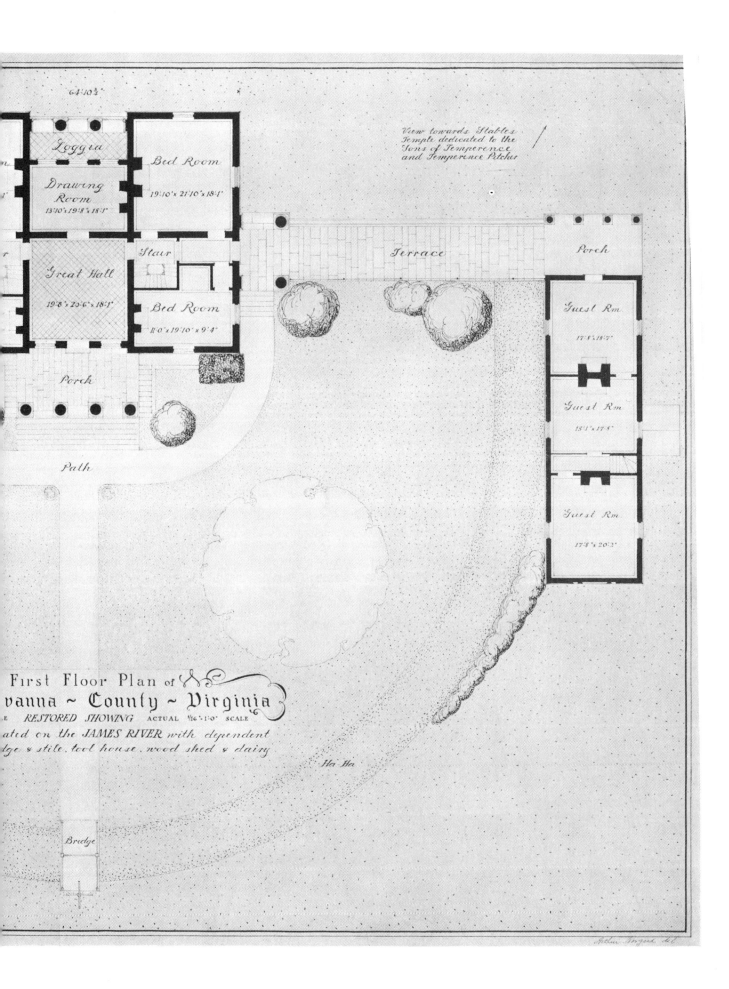

Loggia

Drawing
Room
13'10" x 19'8" x 18'1"

Bed Room
19'10" x 21'10" x 18'1"

Great Hall
19'8" x 25'6" x 18'1"

Stair

Bed Room
11'0" x 19'10" x 9'4"

Porch

Path

64'10½"

View towards Stables
Temple dedicated to the
Sons of Temperence
and Temperence Pitcher

Terrace

Porch

Guest Rm
17'8" x 18'7"

Guest Rm
15'1" x 17'8"

Guest Rm
17'8" x 20'2"

First Floor Plan of
vanna ~ County ~ Virginia
RESTORED SHOWING ACTUAL ⅛"=1'0" SCALE
ated on the JAMES RIVER with dependent
dge & stile, tool house, wood shed & dairy

Ha Ha

Bridge

97

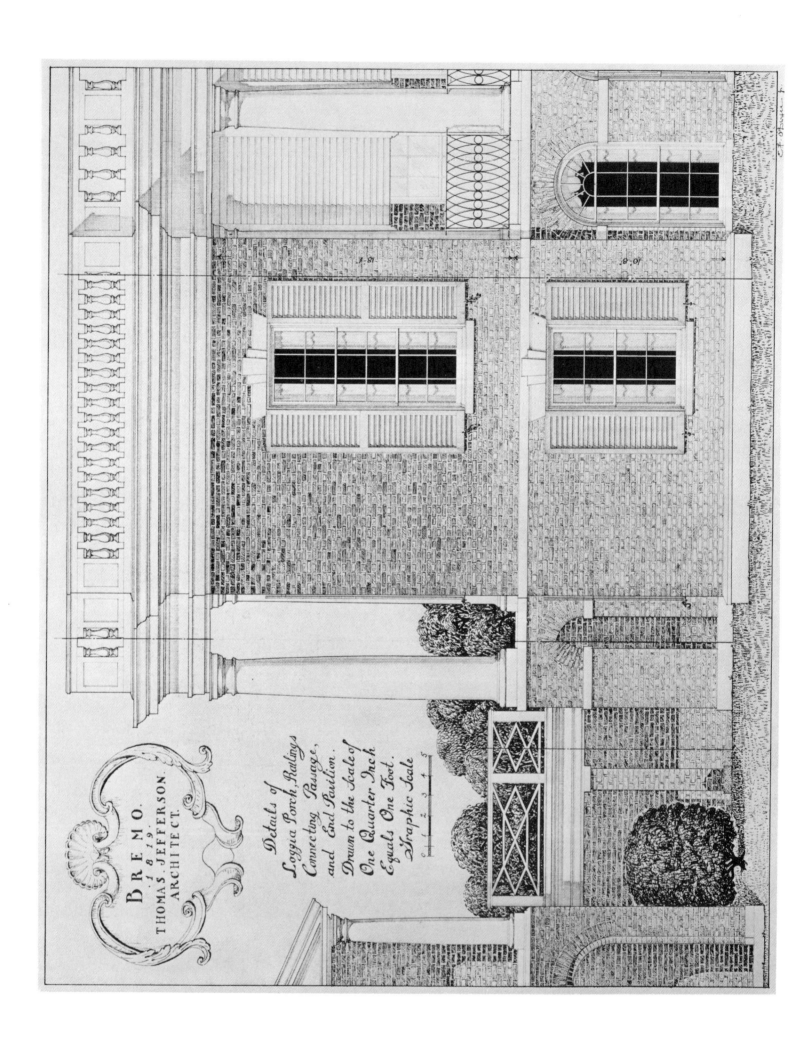

BREMO.
1819.
THOMAS. JEFFERSON.
ARCHITECT.

Details of
Loggia Porch, Railings
Connecting Passage,
and End Pavilion.
Drawn to the scale of
One Quarter Inch
Equals One Foot.
Graphic Scale

TEMPERANCE~TEMPLE

~At BREMO Fluvanna County Virginia Built By General COCKE ~1841~
~ Drawn To The Scale of One Quarter Inch Equals One Foot ~

~ Graphic Scale ~

~DETAIL~OF~
Temperance
Pitcher
Made of Cast Iron

DEDICATED
to the SONS of
TEMPERANCE

The South
Bremo ~ Fluva...

THE CONDITIONS *after roo...*
railing added ty Gen...
graphic scale '...

Facsimile from Diary of General John Hartwell Cocke

Sept. 19. Commenced taking off Roof of the house
to be replaced by a new one, to get rid of the
evils of flat roofing & spouts & gutters - or in other
words, to supersede the deformance by the Com-
- mon Sense plan..

acade of
nty ~ Virginia
G
'op balustrade and roof
TWELL COCKE in 1836
⁵⁄₁₆:1'·0' actual scale

Transcript of facsimile from Diary of General John Hartwell Cocke

Sept. 19, 1836. Commenced taking off Roof of the House to be replaced by a new one, to get rid of the evils of flat roofing and spouts and gutters—or in other words, to supersede the Jeffersonian by the Common Sense Plan.

Photograph by I. T. Frary

THE DEPENDENCIES AND SERVICE WING

Photograph by Homeier-Clark Studio

THE STABLE

The stable was originally stuccoed. The stalls and interior woodwork are made of solid black walnut

BREMO, FLUVANNA COUNTY, VIRGINIA

Photograph by Frances Benjamin Johnston

BRANDON, PRINCE GEORGE COUNTY, VIRGINIA—THE FAÇADE FACING THE RIVER

Tradition dates the left wing about the middle of the 17th Century and the central building as built by Nathaniel Harrison in the latter half of the 18th Century. The designation "Lower Brandon" was made by the river captains in the 19th Century to differentiate the landing from Upper Brandon. The present owner, Robert W. Daniel, is a descendant of the original owner, Captain John Martin, to whom the original grant was made in 1617

THE Manor is located on the JAMES RIVER and faces WESTOVER. THE SOUTHEAST WING dates from 1712 while the SOUTHWEST WING is of a later date. THE CENTRAL PORTION is said to follow the architectural design of Thomas Jefferson. THE HOUSE was ruthlessly damaged during the CIVIL WAR but has recently been carefully restored. THE PORCHES are also restorations.

LOWE
Prince
SCALE OF ELEVATIO

Lower Brandon was built about the year 1712 by NATHANIEL HARRISON II. It had remained in the possession of his descendants until 1926 when it was bought by MR. ROBERT DANIEL. The red brick WALLS are laid up in Flemish bond and the white wooden CORNICES are enriched by carved modillions. THE ROOFS are of shingles and the SHUTTERS are dark green.

Carl Rudy del.

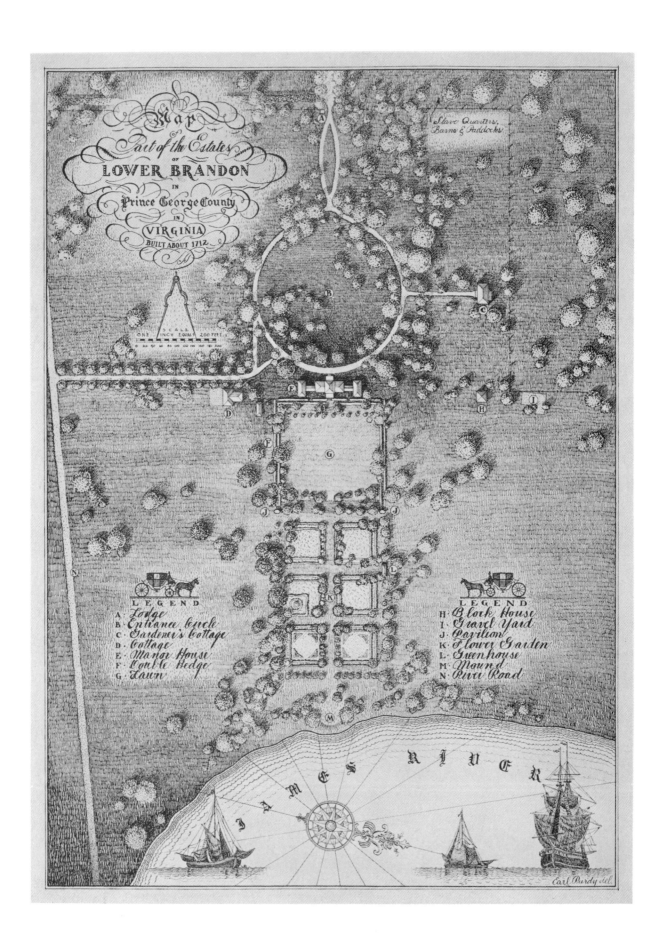

Map
of
Part of the Estates
of
LOWER BRANDON
in
Prince George County
in
VIRGINIA
BUILT ABOUT 1712

SCALE
ONE INCH EQUALS 200 FEET.

Slave Quarters,
Barns & Paddocks

LEGEND
A Lodge
B Entrance Circle
C Gardener's Cottage
D Cottage
E Manor House
F Double Hedge
G Lawn

LEGEND
H Block House
I Gravel Yard
J Pavilion
K Flower Garden
L Green house
M Mound
N River Road

JAMES RIVER

Earl Purdy del.

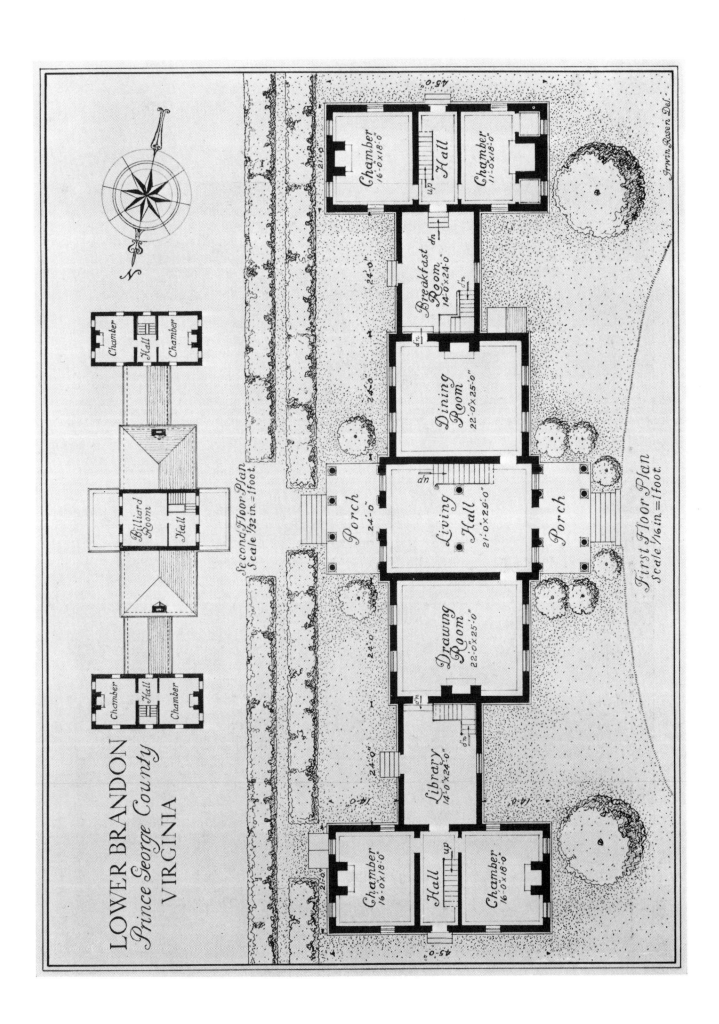

LOWER BRANDON
Prince George County
VIRGINIA

N

Chamber | Hall | Chamber

Billiard Room | Hall

Chamber | Hall | Chamber

Second Floor Plan
Scale 1/32 in.=1 foot

Chamber
16'-0"x18'-0"

Hall

Chamber
11'-0"x18'-0"

Breakfast
Room
14'-0"x24'-0"

Dining
Room
22'-0"x25'-0"

Porch
24'-0"

Living
Hall
21'-0"x29'-0"

Porch

Drawing
Room
22'-0"x25'-0"

Library
14'-0"x24'-0"

Chamber
16'-0"x18'-0"

Hall

Chamber
16'-0"x18'-0"

First Floor Plan
Scale 1/16 in.=1 foot

Irwin Rosen Del.

BRANDON, PRINCE GEORGE COUNTY, VIRGINIA

Mantel and overmantel of the Drawing Room before the restoration

BRANDON, PRINCE GEORGE COUNTY, VIRGINIA
Chippendale Stairway of Connecting Wing

KENMORE, FREDERICKSBURG, VIRGINIA—THE FAÇADE AND PORCH

CORNICE AND CEILING PROFILE

HALF PLAN OF LIBRARY CEILING

Graphic ┣━━━1━━━2━━━3━━━4━━━5 FT. Scale

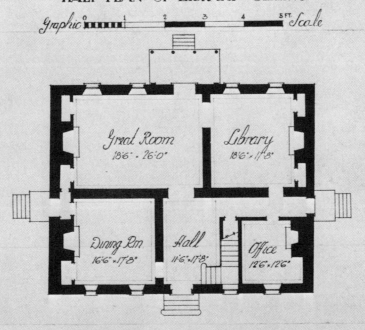

FIRST FLOOR PLAN

Graphic 0━5━10━━20━━30━━40 FT. Scale

Kenmore, Fredericksburg, Virginia
Built in 1753 by Colonel FIELDING LEWIS who
married BETTY, eldest sister of GEORGE WASHINGTON

HALF PLAN OF DINING ROOM CEILING

QUARTER PLAN OF GREAT ROOM CEILING

Graphic ┃┃┃┃┃┃┃ 1 2 3 4 5 6 Scale

Kenmore, Fredericksburg, Virginia

Built in 1753 by Colonel FIELDING LEWIS who
married BETTY, eldest sister of GEORGE WASHINGTON

Paul A. Singer del.

MANTEL SOUTH WALL LIBRARY   MANTEL NORTH WALL GREAT RM.

Graphic 0 1 2 3 4 5FT Scale

Kenmore. Fredericksburg. Virginia

Built in 1753 by Colonel FIELDING LEWIS who
married BETTY, eldest sister of GEORGE WASHINGTON

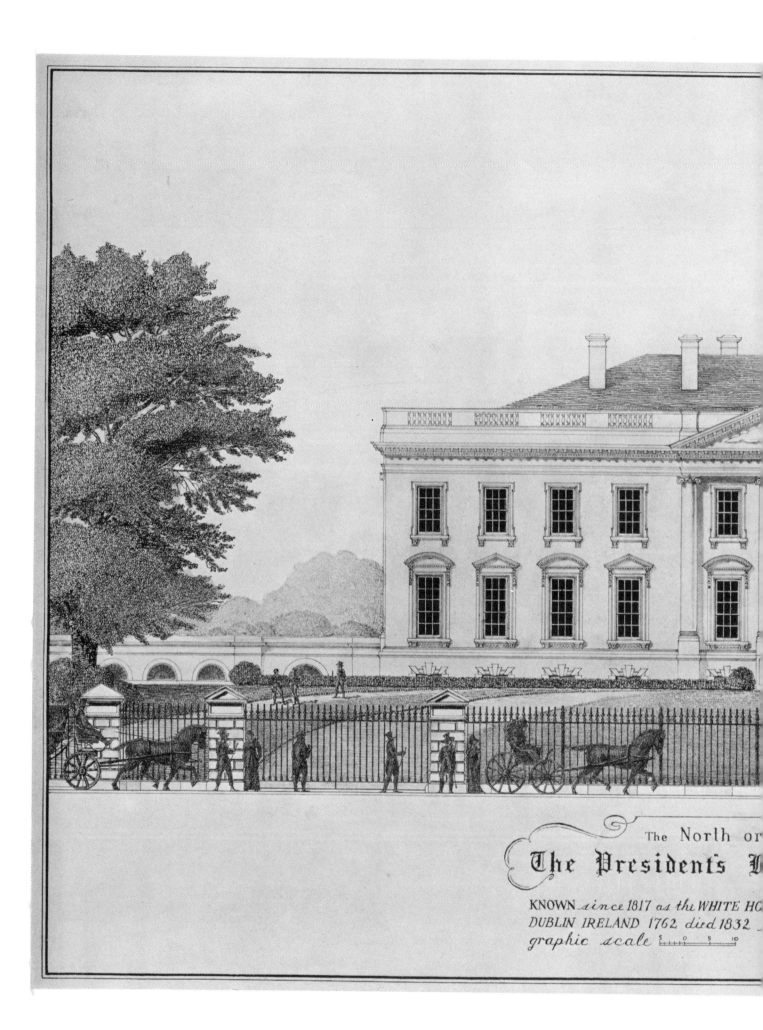

The North or

The President's

KNOWN since 1817 as the WHITE HO
DUBLIN IRELAND 1762 died 1832
graphic scale

John Loughnane Del.

...nce Façade of

...e – Washington D.C.

...323

...the design of JAMES HOBAN born in

...t PORTE COCHERE was added in 1829

1/16"=1'-0" actual scale

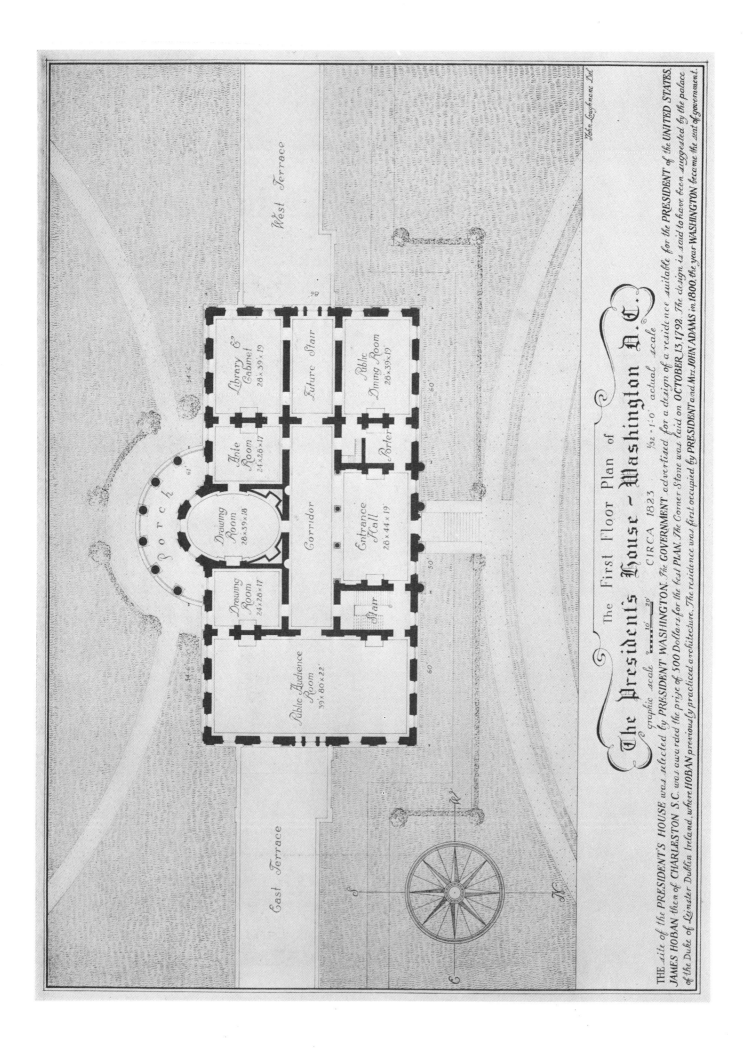

The First Floor Plan of

The President's House ~ Washington D.C.

CIRCA 1823

graphic scale ¹/₃₂ = 1'.0' actual scale

THE site of the PRESIDENT'S HOUSE was selected by PRESIDENT WASHINGTON. The GOVERNMENT advertised for a design of a residence suitable for the PRESIDENT of the UNITED STATES. JAMES HOBAN then of CHARLESTON S.C. was awarded the prize of 500 Dollars for the best PLAN. The Corner Stone was laid on OCTOBER 13, 1792. The design is said to have been suggested by the palace of the Duke of Leinster Dublin Ireland, where HOBAN previously practiced architecture. The residence was first occupied by PRESIDENT and Mr.JOHN ADAMS in 1800, the year WASHINGTON became the seat of government.

John Loughman Del.

West Terrace

East Terrace

Library & Cabinet 28×39×19

Future Stair

Public Dining Room 26×39×19

Ante Room 24×28×17

Porter

Drawing Room 28×39×18

Corridor

Entrance Hall 26×44×19

Drawing Room 24×28×17

Stair

Public Audience Room 39×80×22

Porch

The East Facade of

The President's House ~ Washington D.C.

CIRCA 1823   ⅛″= 1′-0″   actual   scale

graphic scale 0 ‥‥‥ 10   20

John Loughran Del.

THOMAS JEFFERSON himself an Architect of parts, while PRESIDENT made many improvements to the PRESIDENT'S HOUSE He designed and had built the Terraces in order to accommodate the clerical offices, stables and servants quarters. Also during His administration 1801~09 the grounds were leveled and enclosed with an iron and stone wall. During the WAR of 1812 while JAMES MADISON was PRESIDENT 1809~17 the PRESIDENT'S HOUSE was seriously damaged by fire. HOBAN supervised the rebuilding 1815~17. The fire stained walls of Sandstone were thereupon painted White.

The South or

𝕿𝖍𝖊 𝕻𝖗𝖊𝖘𝖎𝖉𝖊𝖓𝖙𝖘 𝕳

CL

THOMAS JEFFERSON *sketched the sem*

was built in 1829 The TERRACES were des

graphic scale

n Façade of

~ Washington D.C.

r porch on HOBAN'S original plan, it
built by PRESIDENT JEFFERSON 1801-09
1/16=1'-0" actual scale

John Loughnane Del.

ENTRANCE FAÇADE, SHOWING THE BOX PARTERRE OF TUDOR PLACE, GEORGETOWN, D. C.

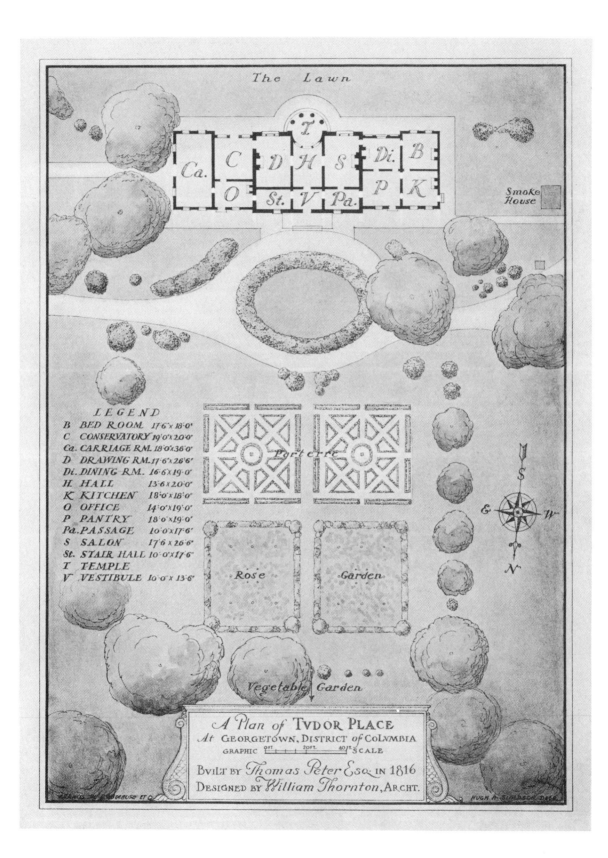

The Lawn

Ca. | C | D | H | S | Di. | B
O | St. | V | Pa. | P | K

T

Smoke House

LEGEND

B   BED ROOM   17'6" x 18'0"
C   CONSERVATORY   19'0" x 20'0"
Ca. CARRIAGE RM. 18'0" x 36'0"
D   DRAWING RM. 17'6" x 26'6"
Di. DINING RM. 16'6" x 19'0"
H   HALL   13'6" x 20'0"
K   KITCHEN   18'0" x 18'0"
O   OFFICE   14'0" x 19'0"
P   PANTRY   18'0" x 19'0"
Pa. PASSAGE   10'0" x 17'6"
S   SALON   17'6" x 26'6"
St. STAIR HALL 10'0" x 17'6"
T   TEMPLE
V   VESTIBULE 10'0" x 13'6"

Parterre

Rose   Garden

Vegetable Garden

A Plan of TVDOR PLACE
At GEORGETOWN, DISTRICT of COLVMBIA
GRAPHIC 0FT.   20FT.   40FT. SCALE
BVILT BY Thomas Peter Esq. IN 1816
DESIGNED BY William Thornton, ARCHT.

·The South FACADE from the River·

Graphic   Scale

Tu[...]
G[...]
DISTRI[...]

Built by Thomas Peter Esquire
in 1816
William Thornton, Architect

FRANCIS W. ROUDEBUSH DEL.

Photograph by Frances Benjamin Johnston

TEMPLE PORTICO OF THE GARDEN FAÇADE OF TUDOR PLACE,
GEORGETOWN, D. C.

Photograph by Frances Benjamin Johnston

DETAIL OF DRAWING ROOM OF TUDOR PLACE, GEORGETOWN, D. C.

·THE·SOUTH·OR
★ ★ DUMBAR
Georgetown ~

THE ORIGINAL HOUSE *was built before 1751 by GE*
NOURSE sold the property to CHARLES CARROLL, cousin
name of "BELLEVUE" ~ In 1915 the house was moved
Graphic

NCE · FACADE · OF ·

★ HOUSE ★

t of Columbia

built in 1805 in its present form by JOSEPH NOURSE - In 1815
he Declaration of Independence , who gave the house the
he NATIONAL SOCIETY of the COLONIAL DAMES of AMERICA
⌐⌐ Scale

Wallace Heath, del.

GARDEN FAÇADE OF DUMBARTON HOUSE, GEORGETOWN, D. C.

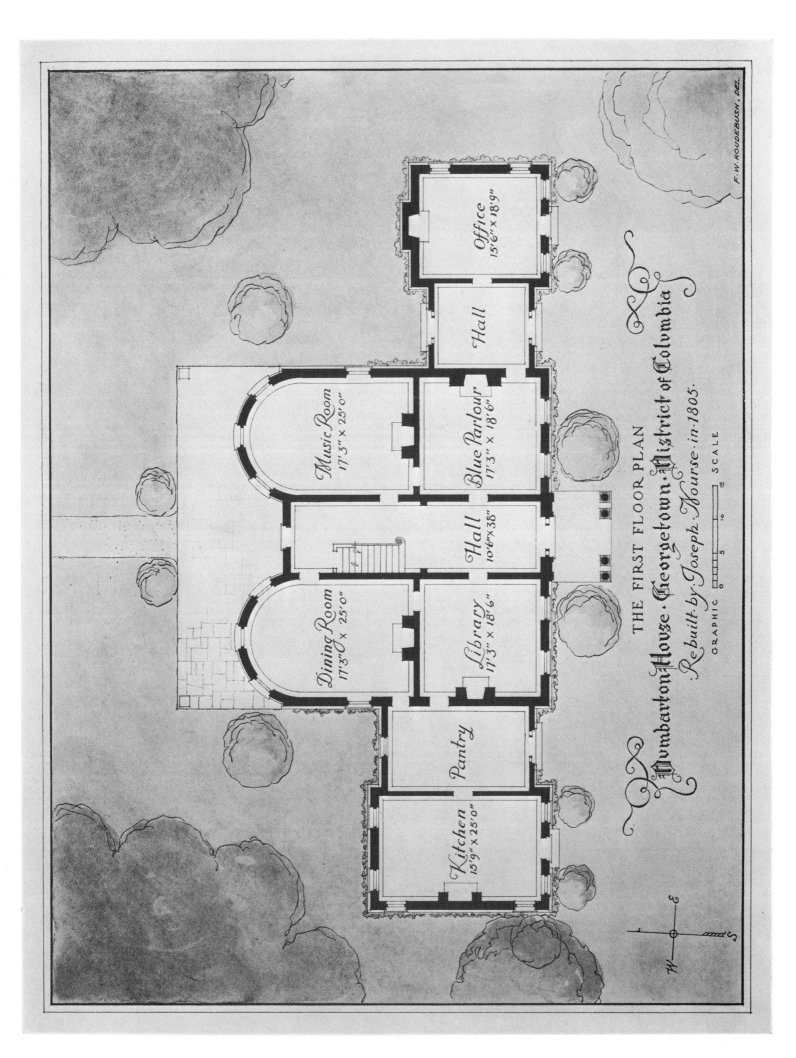

THE FIRST FLOOR PLAN

Dumbarton House · Georgetown · District of Columbia

Rebuilt by · Joseph Nourse · in 1805 ·

F. W. ROUDEBUSH , DEL.

Office
15'6" x 18'9"

Hall

Music Room
17'3" x 25'0"

Blue Parlour
17'3" x 18'6"

Hall
10'6"x38"

Dining Room
17'0" x 25'0"

Library
17'3" x 18'6"

Pantry

Kitchen
15'9" x 25'0"

GRAPHIC SCALE
0   5   10   15

Photograph by Frances Benjamin Johnston

THE LIBRARY OF DUMBARTON HOUSE, GEORGETOWN, D. C.

· INTERIOR · CORNICES ·
DUMBARTON · HOUSE · GEORGETOWN · D · C ·
SCALE: 1/8 INCH EQUALS 1 INCH   WALLACE HEATH DEL.

GARDEN FAÇADE OF DOUGHOREGAN MANOR, HOWARD COUNTY, MARYLAND

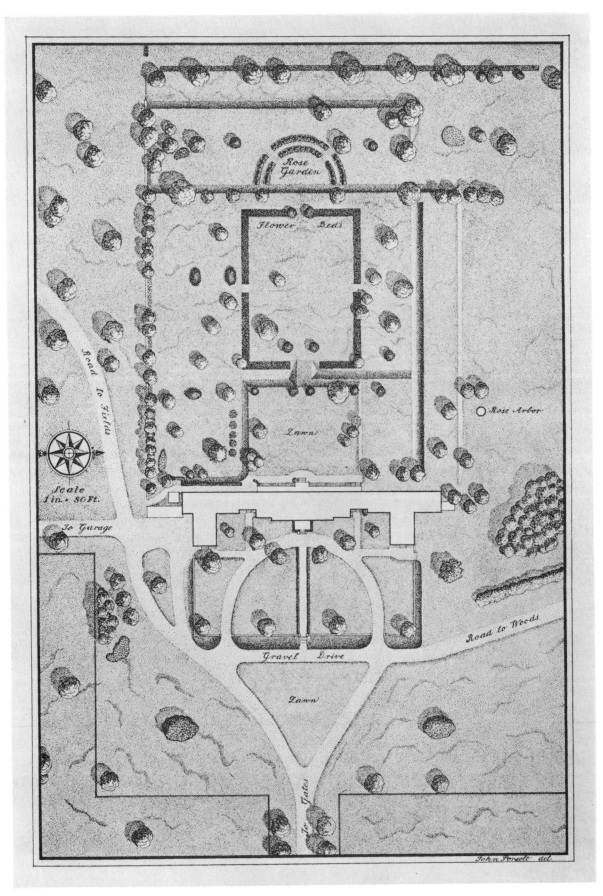

Rose
Garden

Flower Beds

Road to Fields

○ Rose Arbor

Lawn

Scale
1 in. = 80 Ft.

To Garage

Road to Woods

Gravel Drive

Lawn

To Gates

John Pinsole del.

The GARDEN PLAN of
DOUGHOREGAN MANOR
Howard County   Maryland

133

DOUGHORE

HOWARD

Lived in by Charle
Who was born in
NOW OWNE

Scale ⊢━━━━ 5   10   15   20 Fut

N   MANOR

Y · MARYLAND

rroll of   Carrollton
and died in 1832

HILIP CARROLL

E H Sammons, Del.

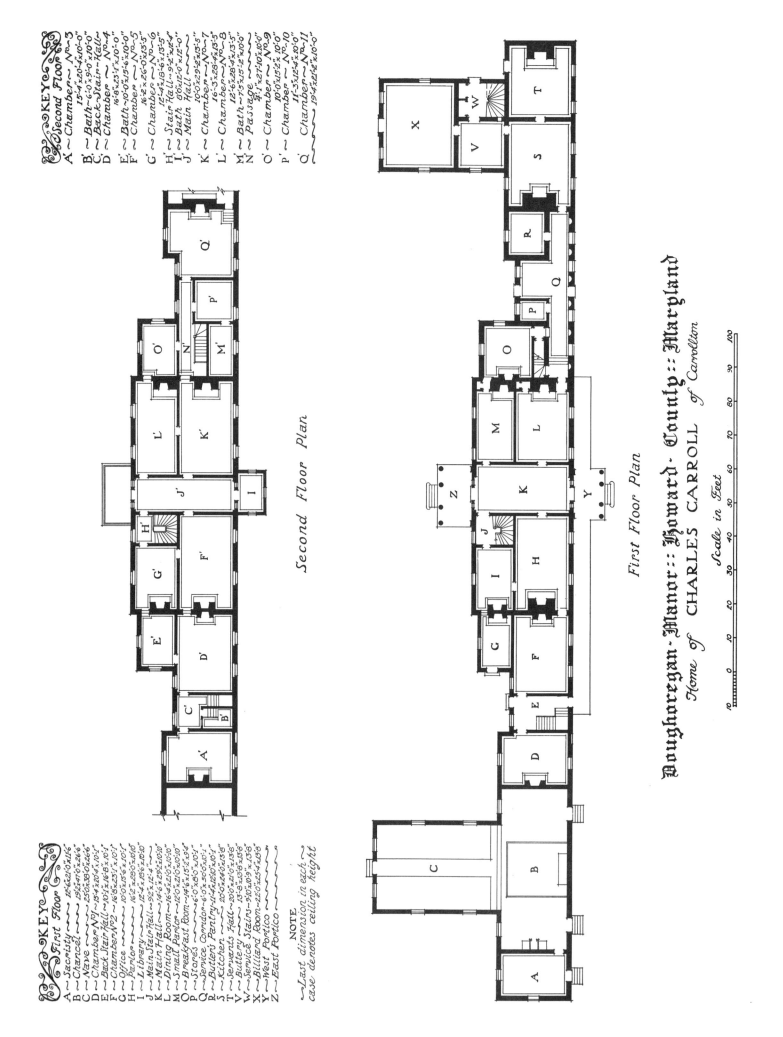

KEY
Second Floor

A´ ~ Chamber ~ Nº 3 ~ 12'6½"x20'4"x10'6"
B´ ~ Bath ~ 6'0"x9'-0"x10'-0"
C´ ~ Back Stair Hall ~
D´ ~ Chamber ~ Nº 4 ~ 16'-8"x25'-1"x10'-0"
E´ ~ Bath ~ 10'-0"x15'-6"x10'-0"
F´ ~ Chamber ~ Nº 5 ~ 16'-2"x26'-0"x13'-5"
G´ ~ Chamber ~ Nº 6 ~ 12'-4"x18'-6"x13'-5"
H´ ~ Stair Hall ~ 9'-2"x24'
I´ ~ Bath ~ 8'0"x12'-0"x10'-0"
J´ ~ Main Hall ~ 10'-0"x29'-2"x13'-5"
K´ ~ Chamber ~ Nº 7 ~ 16'-3"x28'-4"x13'-5"
L´ ~ Chamber ~ Nº 8 ~ 12'-6"x28'-4"x13'-5"
M´ ~ Bath ~ 7'-5"x15'-4"x10'-0"
N´ ~ Passage ~ 4'-1"x27'-10"x10'-0"
O´ ~ Chamber ~ Nº 9 ~ 10'-0"x15'-2"x10'-0"
P´ ~ Chamber ~ Nº 10 ~ 11'-3½"x14'-0"x10'-0"
Q´ ~ Chamber ~ Nº 11 ~ 19'-4"x21'-2"x10'-0"

Second Floor Plan

KEY
First Floor

A ~ Sacristy ~ 12'6½"x10'11½"
B ~ Chancel ~ 19'2"x10'x26'6
C ~ Nave ~ 25'0"x38'-0"x26'6
D ~ Chamber Nº 1 ~ 15'-4"x20'4"x10'1"
E ~ Back Stair Hall ~ 10'1"x16'-8"x10'1"
F ~ Chamber Nº 2 ~ 16'-8"x25'-1"x10'1"
G ~ Office ~ 10'-0"x15'-6"x10'-0"
H ~ Parlor ~ 16'2"x29'-6"x10'6
I ~ Library ~ 12'-4"x18'-6"x10'-10"
J ~ Main Stair Hall ~ 9'2"x12'-4"
K ~ Main Hall ~ 14'6"x29'-2"x10'10"
L ~ Small Parlor ~ 16'0"x21'-0"x10'-10"
M ~ Breakfast Room ~ 14'6"x15'-2"x9'4
N ~ Stores ~ 10'-0"x29'-2"x10'-5"
O ~ Service Corridor ~ 6'-0"x56'-0"x10'-1"
P ~ Butler's Pantry ~ 11'4"x13'-0"x10'-1"
Q ~ Kitchen ~ 20'6"x24'-0"x13'8
R ~ Servants Hall ~ 20'5"x21'-0"x13'8
S ~ Butlery ~ 13'-6"x13'-8"x13'8
T ~ Service Stairs ~ 9'10"x10'9"x13'8
V ~ Billiard Room ~ 22'0"x25'-4"x13'8
W ~ West Portico ~
Y ~ East Portico ~
Z ~ East Portico ~

NOTE
~ Last dimension in each
case denotes ceiling height

First Floor Plan

Scale in Feet

Doughoregan Manor :: Howard County :: Maryland
Home of CHARLES CARROLL of Carrollton

Eugene B. Fetterell, Del.

ENTRANCE FAÇADE OF DOUGHOREGAN MANOR, HOWARD COUNTY, MARYLAND, SHOWING THE WINGS OF THE CHAPEL AND BILLIARD ROOM

Photograph by J. H. Schaefer & Son.

ENTRANCE FAÇADE OF HOMEWOOD, BALTIMORE, MARYLAND

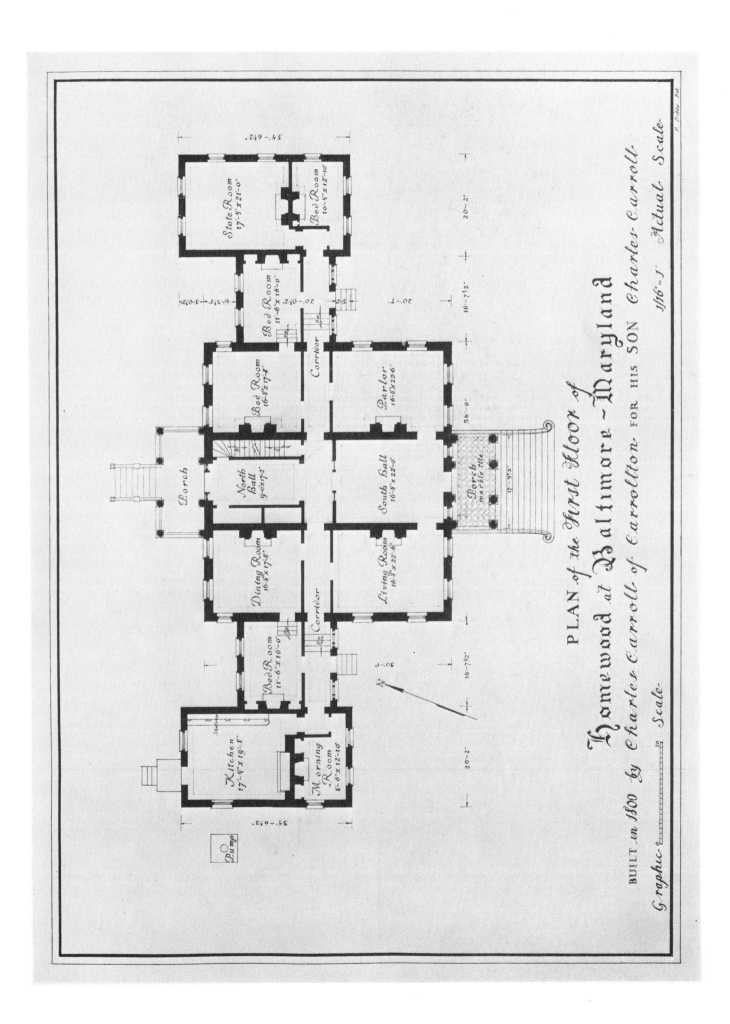

PLAN of the First Floor of

Homewood at Baltimore ~ Maryland

BUILT in 1800 by Charles Carroll of Carrollton FOR HIS SON Charles Carroll.

Graphic Scale.   1/16=1' Actual Scale.

SOUT[H]

HOMEWOOD *was built
during the year 1800
The name of the builder
was William Edwards*

ATION

E. H. Sammons. Del.

HOMEWOOD *was built by*
Charles Carroll of Carrollton
who was a signer of The
Declaration of Independence

DETAIL of SOUTH ELEVATION

Homewood Baltimore~Maryland

DRAWN TO *scale of ¼"=1'-0"*

Mitchell Wooten, Del.

DOORWAY *from* LIVING ROOM *to* CORRIDOR

DOORWAY *of* STATE ROOM

DOORWAY *from* LIVING ROOM *to* SOVTH HALL

MANTEL *in* STATE ROOM

Interior Details
of Homewood *at*
Baltimore~Maryland
BVILT *in* 1809 *by* CHARLES CARROLL
1″=3′ ~ *Actual Scales* ~ 1/2″=1′
Graphic Scales

NORTH

HOMEWOOD *was built*
during the year 1800
The name of the builder
was William Edwards

ATION

E.H. Sammons - Del.

HOMEWOOD *was built by*
Charles Carroll of Carrollton
who was a signer of The
Declaration of Independence

145

TEMPLE PORTICO OF WHITEHALL, ANNE ARUNDEL COUNTY, MARYLAND

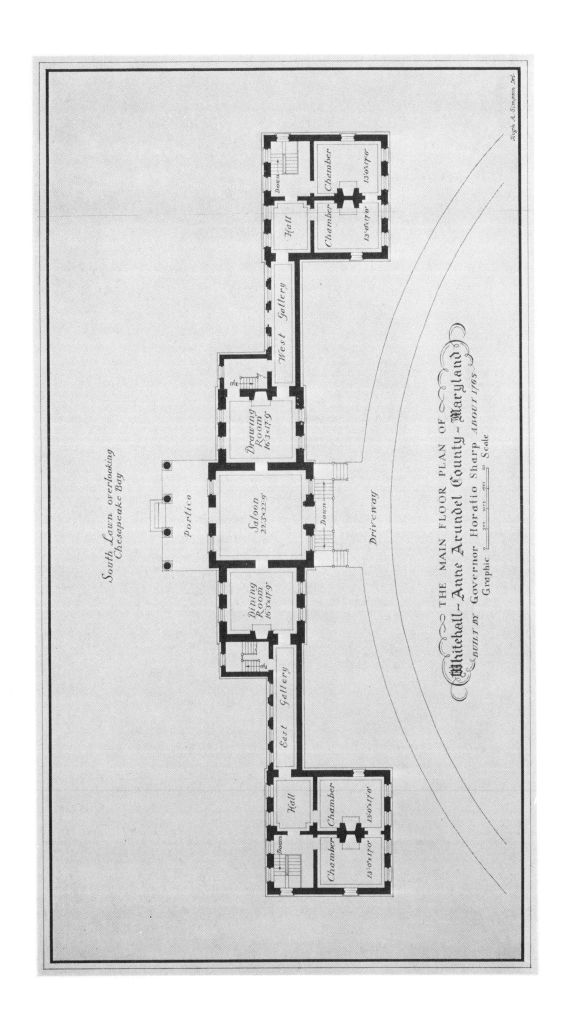

South Lawn overlooking
Chesapeake Bay

portico

Saloon
21′3″x22′9″

Dining Room
16′3″x17′9″

Drawing Room
16′3″x17′9″

West Gallery

East Gallery

Hall

Hall

Chamber
13′0″x17′0″

Chamber
13′0″x17′0″

Chamber
13′0″x17′0″

Chamber
13′0″x17′0″

Down

Down

Down

Driveway

THE MAIN FLOOR PLAN OF
Whitehall~Anne Arundel County~Maryland
BUILT BY Governor Horatio Sharp ABOUT 1765
Graphic   Scale

Hugh A. Simpson Del.

147

THE NORTH o...
Whitehall—Anne A...
BUILT BY Governor
Graphic ...

AY FACADE OF

County-Maryland

Sharp ABOUT 1765

5 ft. 20 Scale

Hugh A. Sampson del

Courtesy of White Pine Series   *Photograph by Kenneth Clark*

INTERIOR OF GREAT HALL OF WHITEHALL, ANNE ARUNDEL
COUNTY, MARYLAND

Courtesy of White Pine Series   *Photograph by Kenneth Clark*

DETAIL OF MANTELPIECE OF WHITEHALL, ANNE ARUNDEL
COUNTY, MARYLAND

Inset: Wooden mask inserted into the cornice of the cove ceiling at Whitehall

DETAIL OF JAMBS
AND SOFFIT

Details of INTERIOR DOOR TRIM & *base*
Whitehall · Anne Arundel County · Maryland

GRAPHIC   0   3   6   9   12   SCALE
INCHES
Hugh A. Simpson Del.

Details of THE MAIN PORTICO *& Window*
Whitehall · Anne Arundel County · Maryland
GRAPHIC SCALE 0 3" 6" 9" 1FT. 2FT. 1½ IN. EQUALS 1 FT.

Hugh A. Simpson Del.

· THE · S

THE · MATTHIAS

· Anna

Built in 1770 · Wil

NOW OWNED BY ST. JOHN

Graphic

...ACADE · ←——————→ · ◎

...MMOND · HOUSE

...aryland ·

...uckland · Architect

...GE AS A COLONIAL MUSEUM

15ᶠᵗ   20ᶠᵗ   Scale

Wallace Heath, del.

GARDEN FAÇADE OF THE MATTHIAS HAMMOND HOUSE, ANNAPOLIS,
MARYLAND

MAIN ENTRANCE DOORWAY OF THE MATTHIAS HAMMOND HOUSE,
ANNAPOLIS, MARYLAND

This is one of the most beautifully executed Georgian doorways in this country

DETAIL OF DOORWAY AND CARVED SHUTTERS OF THE STATE DINING
ROOM, MATTHIAS HAMMOND HOUSE, ANNAPOLIS, MARYLAND

Courtesy of White Pine Series   *Photograph by Kenneth Clark*

MANTEL AND OVERMANTEL IN THE STATE DINING ROOM, MATTHIAS
HAMMOND HOUSE, ANNAPOLIS, MARYLAND

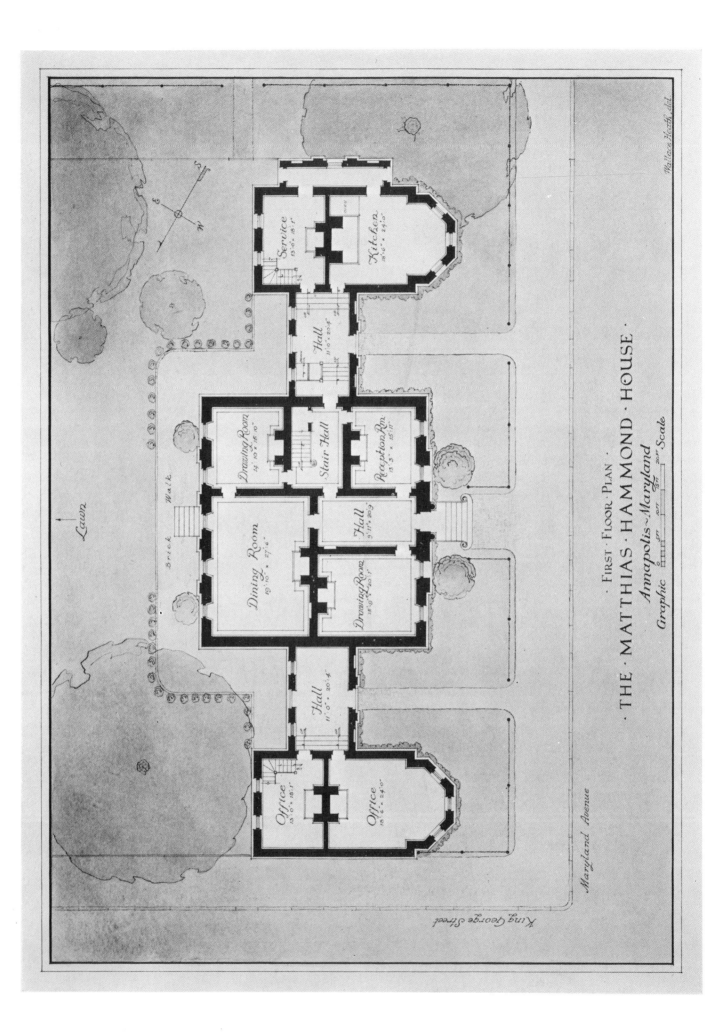

Lawn

Brick Walk

King George Street

Maryland Avenue

Service
13'0"·15'1"

Kitchen
18'6"×24'0"

Hall
11'0"·22'4"

Drawing Room
14'10"·16'0"

Stair Hall

Reception Rm.
13'3"×15'11"

Dining Room
19'10"×27'6"

Hall
9'11"×20'9"

Drawing Room
15'0"·20'5"

Hall
11'0"·20'4"

Office
13'0"·15'1"

Office
18'6"×24'0"

Walter·Heath·del.

·FIRST·FLOOR·PLAN·
·THE·MATTHIAS·HAMMOND·HOUSE·
Annapolis~Maryland
Graphic   Scale
0   5ft   10ft   15ft   20ft

ENTRANCE FAÇADE OF MONTPELIER, PRINCE GEORGES COUNTY, MARYLAND

M---
al...
The SNOW...
Prince Geo...
graphic...
act...

G House
Maryland
scale

Arthur Nörgaard del.

DETAIL OF THE ENTRANCE DOORWAY, MONTPELIER, PRINCE GEORGES
COUNTY, MARYLAND

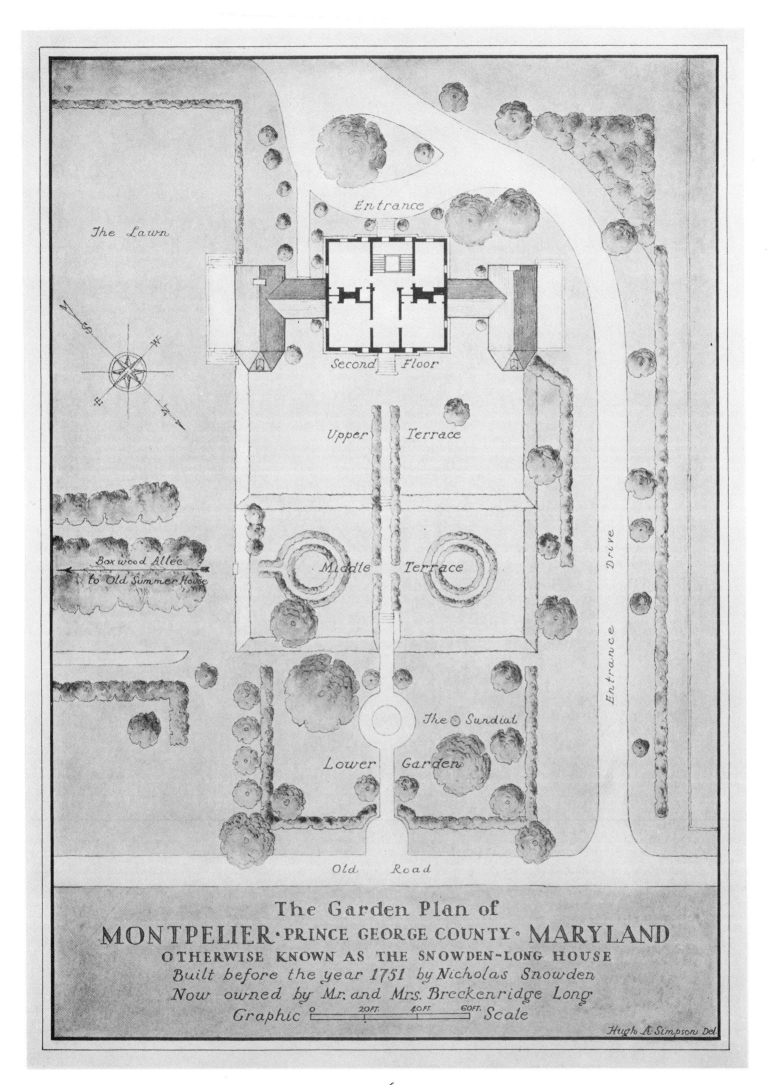

The Lawn

Entrance

Second Floor

Upper Terrace

Boxwood Allée
to Old Summer House

Middle Terrace

Entrance Drive

The Sundial

Lower Garden

Old Road

The Garden Plan of
MONTPELIER · PRINCE GEORGE COUNTY · MARYLAND
OTHERWISE KNOWN AS THE SNOWDEN-LONG HOUSE
Built before the year 1751 by Nicholas Snowden
Now owned by Mr. and Mrs. Breckenridge Long
Graphic ⊢ 20FT. 40FT. 60FT. ⊣ Scale

Hugh A. Simpson Del.

INTERIOR OF THE STAIR HALL OF MONTPELIER, PRINCE GEORGES
COUNTY, MARYLAND

Courtesy of White Pine Series   *Photograph by Kenneth Clark*

DETAIL OF CORNER CUPBOARD, MONTPELIER, PRINCE GEORGES COUNTY,
MARYLAND

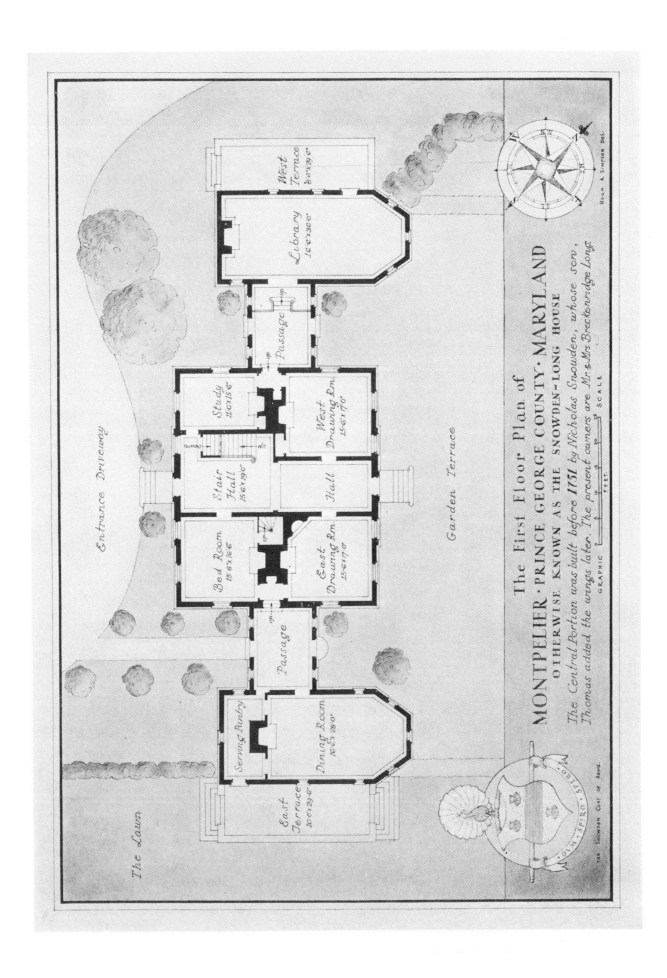

The First Floor Plan of

MONTPELIER · PRINCE GEORGE COUNTY · MARYLAND

OTHERWISE KNOWN AS THE SNOWDEN–LONG HOUSE

The Central Portion was built before 1751 by Nicholas Snowden, whose son,
Thomas added the wings later. The present owners are Mr.s Mr.s Breckenridge Long.

GRAPHIC   SCALE   FEET

Library
16'·6"x36'·0"

West
Terrace
8'·6"x29'·6"

Passage

Study
11'·0"x15'·6"

West
Drawing Rm.
15'·6"x17'·0"

Stair
Hall
15'·6"x19'·0"

Bed Room
15'·6"x16'·6"

Hall

East
Drawing Rm.
15'·6"x17'·0"

Passage

Serving Pantry

Dining Room
16'·0"x28'·0"

East
Terrace
10'·0"x23'·6"

Entrance Driveway

The Lawn

Garden Terrace

THE SNOWDEN COAT OF ARMS.

NVN · SPIRO · SPERO.

HUGH A. SIMPSON DEL.

168

WEST WING, FACING ENTRANCE COURT OF HAMPTON, BALTIMORE
COUNTY, MARYLAND

The South or

Hampton ~ Baltimo

GRAPHIC ⊢⊢⊢⊢⊢ SCALE

THE RESIDENCE *as built by Captain* CHARLES RIDGELY *born 1733 died 1790 He was a private*
had an Architectural Library. It is supposed the main ideas of the design
The central part of the building was the last to be completed. An old reco
winter they were allowed to leave-work at three o'clock so they could avoid

Facade of
ounty ~ Maryland
ACTUAL ⅟₁₆"-1'-0" SCALE

n and the traditions of the family are that he was interested in building and
The house was started in 1783 and completed in 1790 the year of his death.
PTON states that a number of the workmen came from a distance and that in the
r of wolves in travel. The present owner is Capt. John Ridgely of Hampton

Arthur Norgard del.

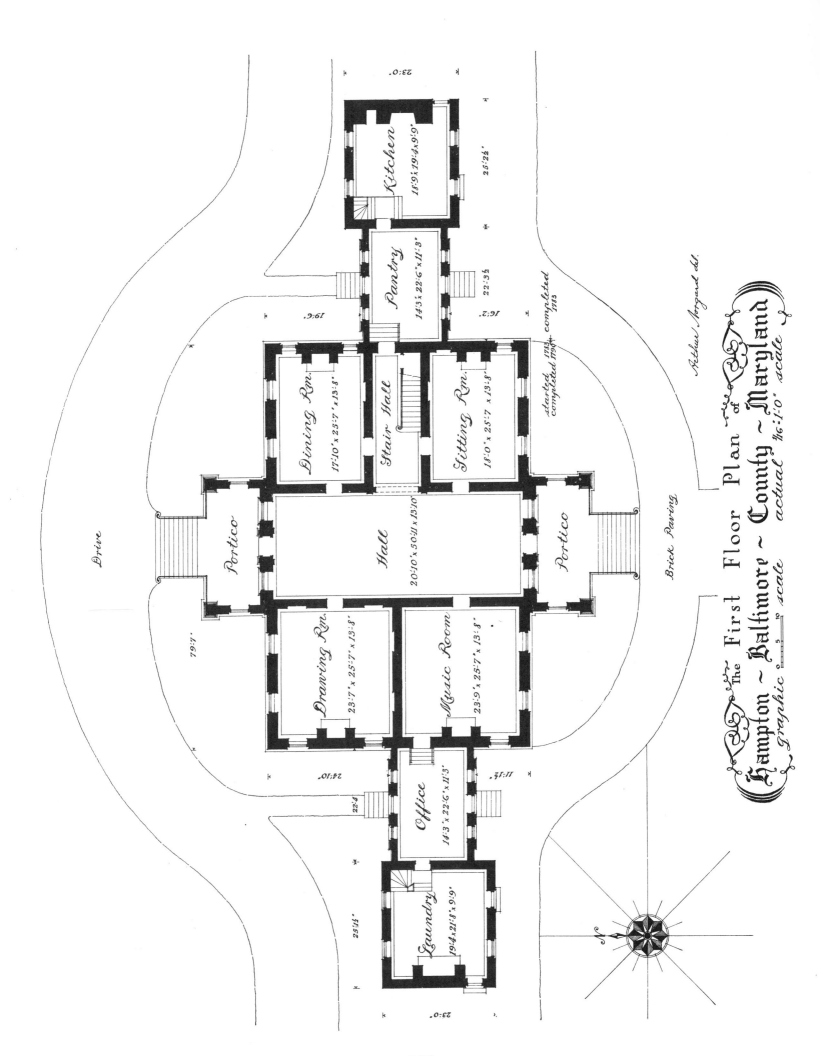

The First Floor Plan of
Hampton ~ Baltimore ~ County ~ Maryland
Graphic scale actual 1/16:1'-0" scale

Arthur Norgard del.

Kitchen
18'-9" x 19'-4" x 9'-9"

Pantry
14'-3" x 22'-6" x 11'-3"

Dining Rm.
17'-10" x 25'-7" x 13'-8"

Stair Hall

Sitting Rm.
18'-0" x 25'-7" x 13'-8"

Portico

Hall
20'-10" x 50'-11" x 13'-10"

Portico

Drawing Rm.
23'-7" x 25'-7" x 13'-8"

Music Room
23'-9" x 25'-7" x 13'-8"

Office
14'-3" x 22'-6" x 11'-3"

Laundry
19'-4" x 21'-8" x 9'-9"

Drive

Brick Paving

started 1783, completed 1783
completed 1790

23'-0"

25'-2½"

22'-3½"

16'-2"

19'-6"

79'-7"

24'-10"

11'-1½"

22'-4"

25'-4"

23'-0"

N

Drive to Entrance Gate

Lawn

Drive to Stables

Entrance Drive

Orangerie

N.

Lawn

Vegetable Garden

Parterre of Box & Flowers

John Orsolt del.

The Garden Plan of
Hampton ~ Baltimore ~ County ~ Maryland
graphic 10 20 30 40 50 60 70 80 90 100 scale

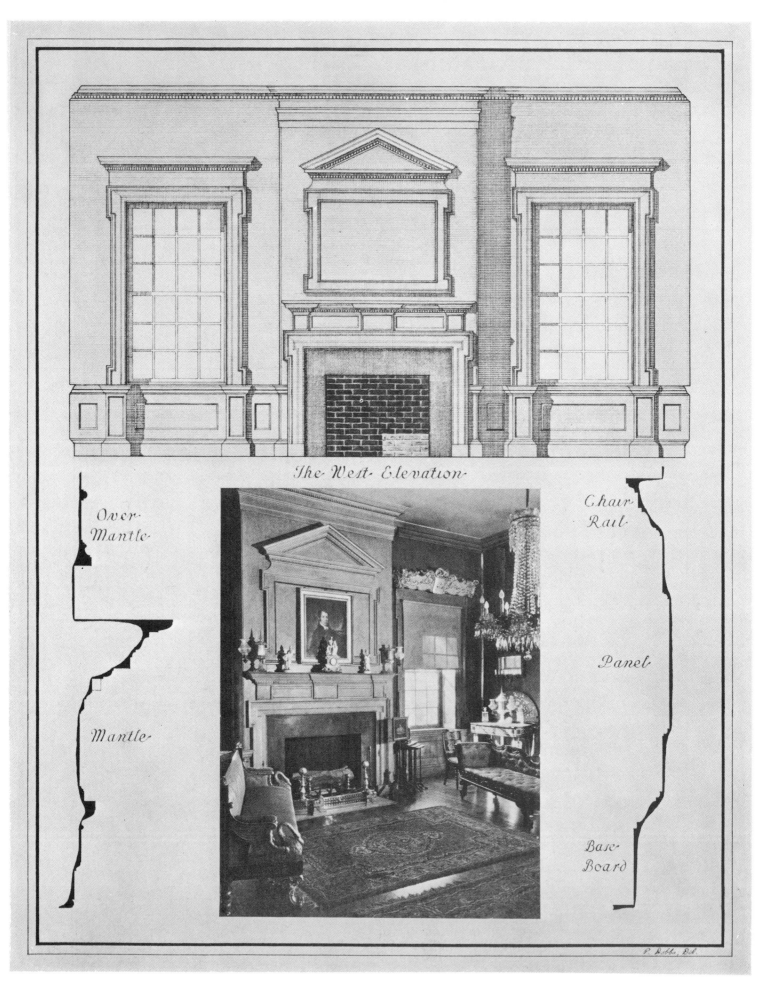

The West Elevation

Over Mantle

Chair Rail

Panel

Mantle

Base Board

P. Dibble, Del.

The *Drawing Room* of
Hampton ~ Baltimore ~ County ~ Maryland
graphic scales inches feet   2"=1' & 1"=3' *actual scales*

The Chimney End of the North~West~Bed~Room

North and South Elevations of the Second~Floor Hall

Interior Details
Hampton ~ Baltimore ~ County ~ Maryland
graphic scale

W. M. Geely Del.

Entrance
Mount Pleasant Mansion
Erected in 1761 by Ca

ade of The
Philadelphia Pennsylvania
n John Macpherson

Scale - 0 [5] 10

ENTRANCE HALL AND STAIRWAY, MOUNT PLEASANT, FAIRMOUNT PARK, PHILADELPHIA, PENNSYLVANIA

THE GREAT CHAMBER, MOUNT PLEASANT, FAIRMOUNT PARK, PHILADELPHIA, PENNSYLVANIA

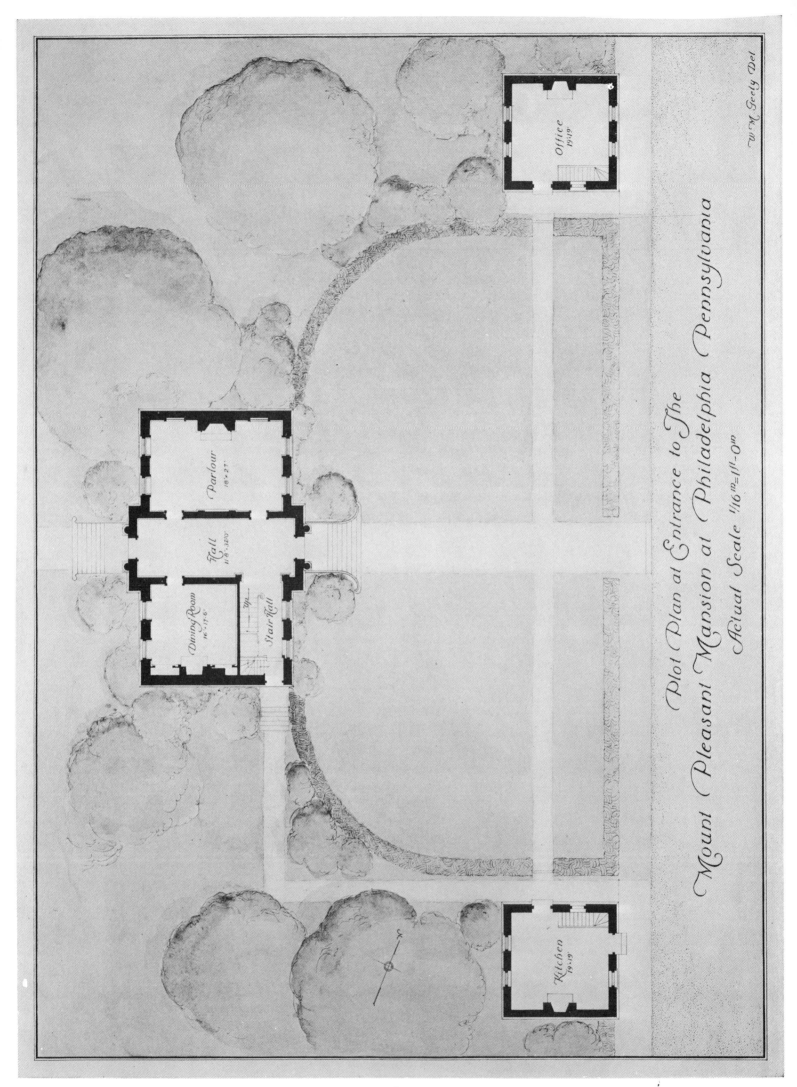

Office
19'19'

Parlour
18'×27'

Hall
11'6'×32'0'

Dining Room
16'×17'6'

Stair Hall

up

Kitchen
19'19'

Plot Plan at Entrance to The

Mount Pleasant Mansion at Philadelphia Pennsylvania

Actual Scale 1/16 in = 1 ft - 0 in

W. M. Seely Del

South Elevation

"Woodlands" House of Andrew Hamilton
Philadelphia Pa.

Wm. Jensen Del.

Built in 1770

Scale ———————— 16 Feet

North Elevation

"Woodlands" House of Andrew Hamilton
Philadelphia Pa.

Wm. Jensen Del.

Built in 1770

Scale ⸻ 16 Feet

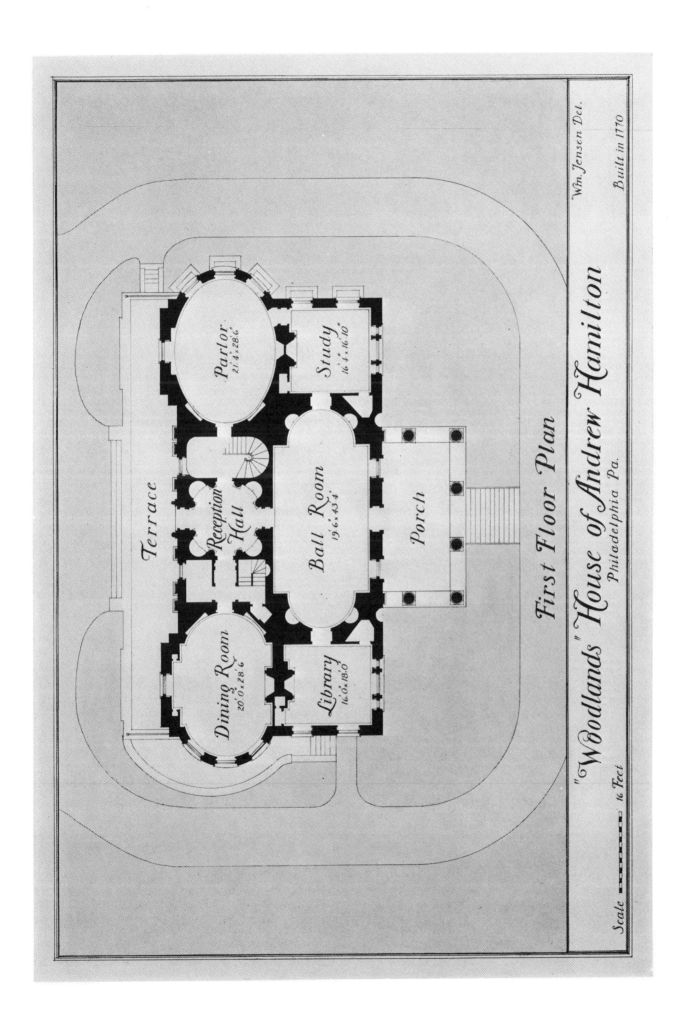

Terrace

Parlor.
21'4"×28'6"

Study
16.4.×16.10.

Reception
Hall

Ball Room
19'.6".×43'.4".

Dining Room
20'.0"×28'.6"

Library
16.0.×18.0.

Porch

First Floor Plan

"Woodlands" House of Andrew Hamilton
Philadelphia Pa.

Wm. Jensen Del.

Built in 1770

Scale ⊢━━━┥ 16 Feet

ENTRANCE FAÇADE OF THE HIGHLANDS, AMBLER, PENNSYLVANIA

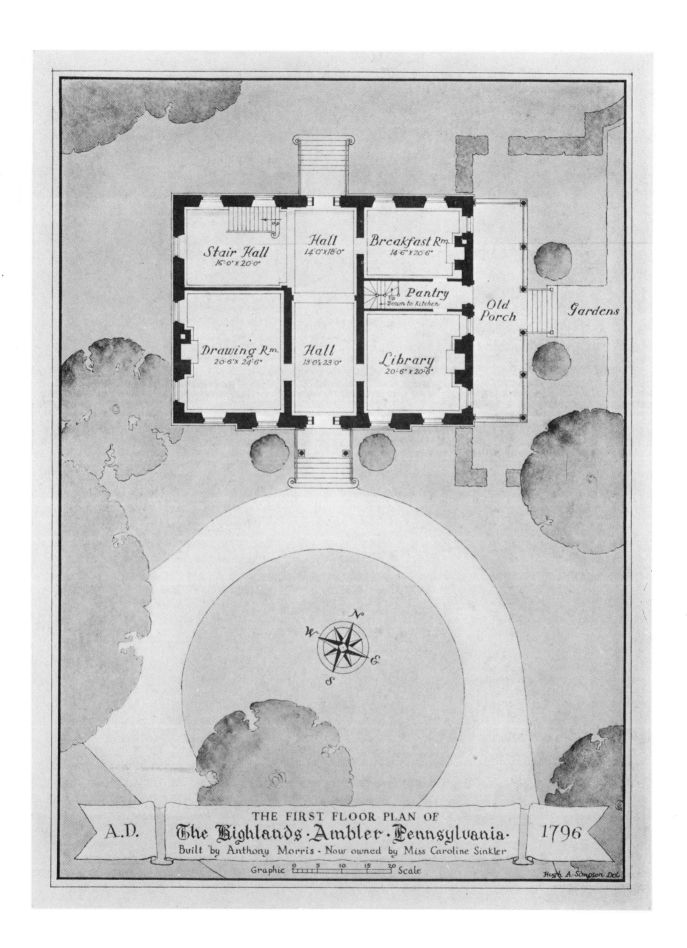

Stair Hall
16'0" x 20'0"

Hall
14'0" x 18'0"

Breakfast R^{m.}
14'6" x 20'6"

Pantry

Up
Down to kitchen

Old Porch

Gardens

Drawing R^{m.}
20'6" x 24'6"

Hall
13'0" x 23'0"

Library
20'6" x 20'0"

N
W E
S

THE FIRST FLOOR PLAN OF
The Highlands · Ambler · Pennsylvania ·
Built by Anthony Morris · Now owned by Miss Caroline Sinkler

A.D.   1796

Graphic 0 5 10 15 20 Scale

Hugh A. Simpson Del.

185

THE CHARLES PHELPS TAFT

...OUSE · CINCINNATI · OHIO

MEASURED · DRAWN · BY · H · RICHARD · ELLISTON · 1935

ENTRANCE PORCH OF CHARLES PHELPS TAFT HOUSE, CINCINNATI, OHIO

Built by Martin Baum in 1820. Purchased by Nicholas Longworth in 1829
and now the Taft Museum

ENTRANCE HALL, CHARLES PHELPS TAFT HOUSE, CINCINNATI, OHIO

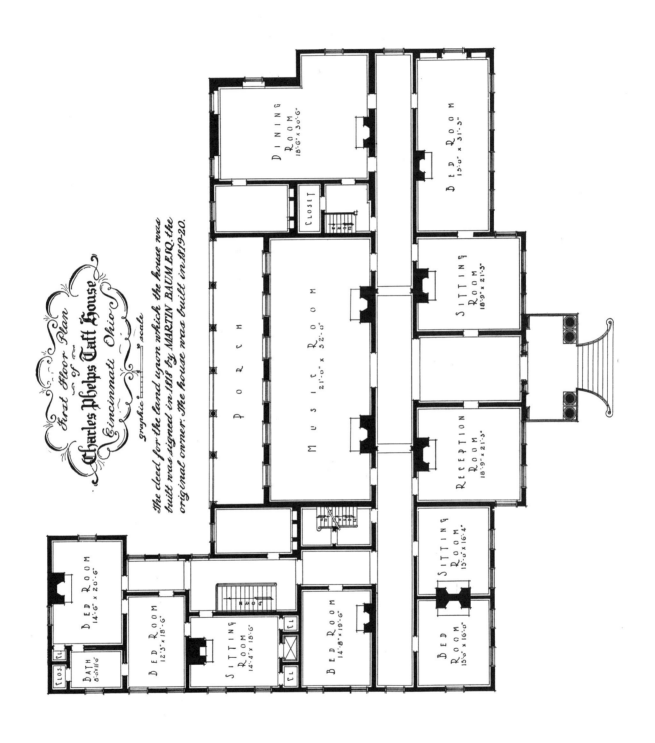

First Floor Plan
of
Charles Phelps Taft House
Cincinnati, Ohio

graphic scale

The deed for the land upon which the house was
built was signed in 1818 by MARTIN BAUM ESQ. the
original owner. The house was built in 1819-20.

DINING ROOM
18'-6" x 30'-6"

CLOSET

BED ROOM
15'-0" x 31'-5"

PORCH

MUSIC ROOM
21'-0" x 52'-0"

SITTING ROOM
18'-9" x 21'-3"

RECEPTION ROOM
18'-9" x 21'-3"

BED ROOM
14'-6" x 20'-6"

CLOS.   CL

BATH
8'-0" x 11'-0"

BED ROOM
12'-3" x 18'-6"

SITTING ROOM
14'-4" x 18'-6"

CL

BED ROOM
14'-8" x 19'-6"

SITTING ROOM
15'-0" x 16'-4"

BED ROOM
15'-0" x 16'-0"

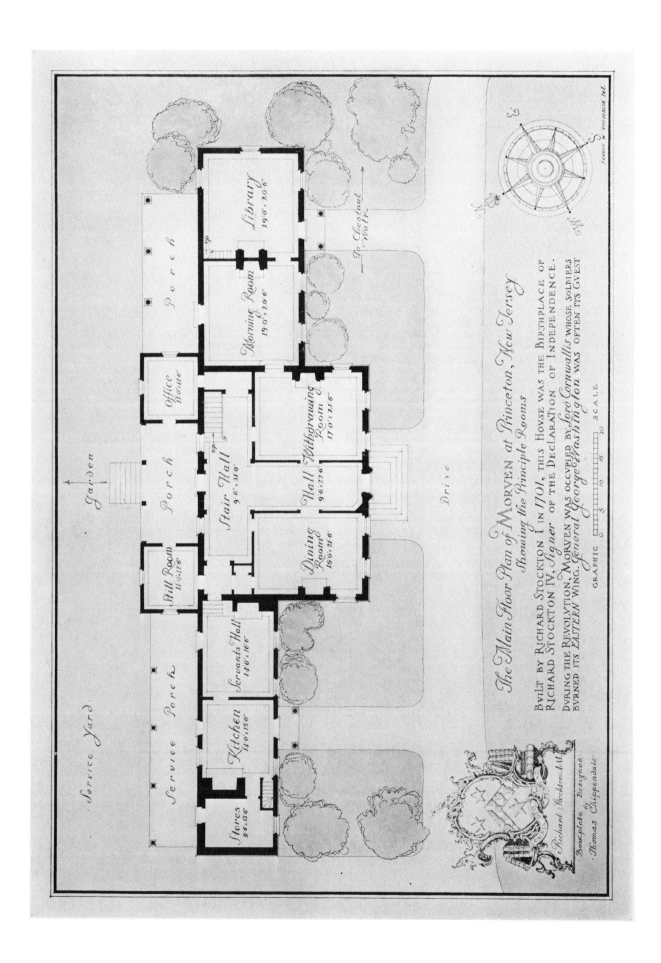

Garden

Service Yard

Service Porch

Porch

Porch

Porch

Stores
9'0"x15'0"

Kitchen
14'0"x15'0"

Servants Hall
14'0"x16'6"

Still Room
11'0"x11'6"

Office
House

Library
19'0"x20'6"

Stair Hall
9'6"x31'0"

Morning Room
19'0"x20'6"

Dining Room
16'0"x21'6"

Hall Withdrawing Room
9'6"x22'6" 17'0"x21'6"

To Chestnut Walk

Drive

Francis W. Rhoadbush Del.

The Main floor Plan of Morven at Princeton, New Jersey
Showing the Principle Rooms

Built by Richard Stockton I in 1701. This House was the Birthplace of
Richard Stockton IV, Signer of the Declaration of Independence.

During the Revolution, Morven was occupied by Lord Cornwallis whose Soldiers
burned its Eastern Wing. General George Washington was often its Guest.

GRAPHIC   0 5 10 5 10 20   SCALE

Richard Stockton A.M.
Bookplate Designed
by
Thomas Chippendale.

191

The South Facade of N
Built by RICHAR
from plan

THIS HOVSE WAS THE BI
Signer of the D

N at *Princeton New Jersey*
TON ESQ. in 1701
n *England*
OF RICHARD STOCKTON IV
of *Independence*

FRANCIS W. ROUDEBUSH DEL.

INTERIOR OF THE MORNING ROOM, MORVEN, PRINCETON, NEW JERSEY

Photograph by Richard Averill Smith

ENTRANCE HALL OF MORVEN, PRINCETON, NEW JERSEY
Built in 1701 by Richard Stockton, remodelled in 1783 and 1788 and again in 1844

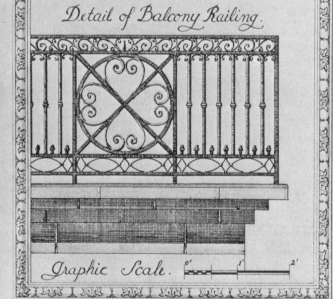

Detail of Balcony Railing.

Graphic Scale.

South
HY
Coop

Built by George Hyde Clark on
the North East is of Brick, and was erec
is of Stone and dates from 1811. The
and was built about 1833. The
ARCHITECT, and are characteristic of
GEORGE CLARK, as a Land Grant pri
mained in that family up to the

196

tion of

HALL
_y._

East Shore of Lake Otsego. The Wing at
_00._ The portion to the West & South West
part to the South East is also of Stone
portions are the work of PHILIP HOOKER
period. The Estate was acquired by,
American Revolution, and has re-
ime.   Graphic ┣━━━━━┫ Scale.

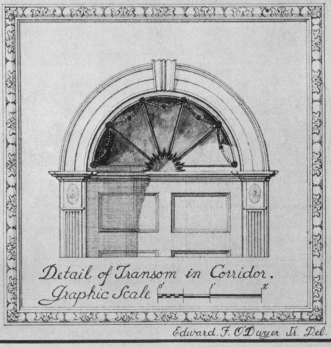

Detail of Transom in Corridor.
Graphic Scale ┣━━━━━━━━━━┫

Edward. F. O'Dwyer Jr. Del.

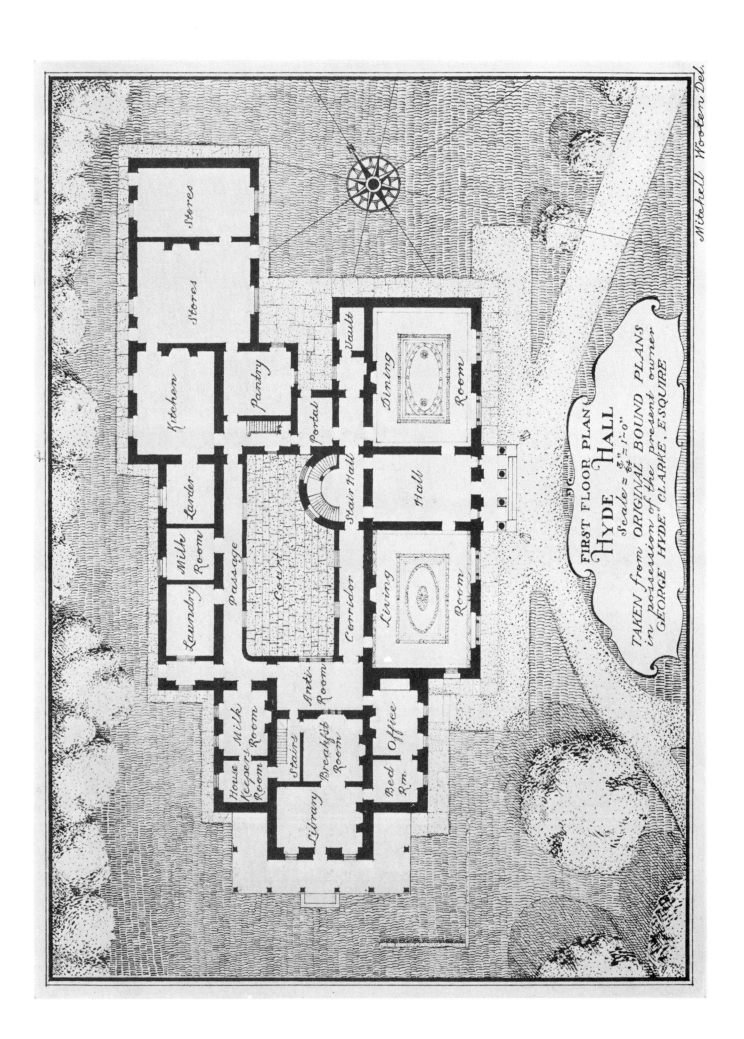

FIRST FLOOR PLAN
HYDE HALL
Scale = 3/64" = 1'-0"

TAKEN from ORIGINAL BOUND PLANS
in possession of the present owner
GEORGE HYDE CLARKE, ESQUIRE

Mitchell Wooten Del.

Stores

Stores

Kitchen

Pantry

Larder

Milk Room

Laundry

Passage

Court

Portal

Vault

Dining Room

Stair Hall

Corridor

Hall

Living Room

House Keeper Room

Milk Room

Stairs

Anti-Room

Breakfast Room

Library

Bed Rm.

Office

198

THE DINING ROOM OF HYDE HALL ON LAKE OTSEGO, NEAR COOPERSTOWN, NEW YORK,
SHOWING A DETAIL OF THE HIGH COVED CEILING

Photograph by Edward Pierrepont Beckwith

DETAIL OF THE MANTELPIECE OF THE LIVING ROOM OF HYDE HALL,
ON LAKE OTSEGO, NEAR COOPERSTOWN, NEW YORK

DETAIL OF THE MANTELPIECE OF THE DINING ROOM, HYDE HALL ON
LAKE OTSEGO, NEAR COOPERSTOWN, NEW YORK

The woodbox to the left of the fireplace is filled from a small door opening into the corridor behind

The Garden or River Facade of
The Van Rensselaer—Manor House—Albany—New York

Scale = 1/16" = 1'-0"

As it stood in 1820. Built in 1765 by the patroon STEPHEN VAN RENSSELAER under the direction of his guardian GENERAL TEN BROECK. The flanking WINGS designed by PHILIP HOOKER were added in 1820. The HOUSE was so remodeled in 1843 by UPJOHN that little of its eighteenth century character remained. The HOUSE was later removed to WILLIAMSTOWN MASSACHUSSETTS where it now stands.

Mitchell Wooten Del.

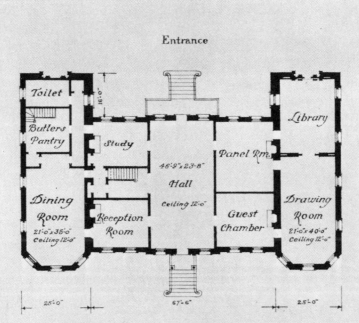

Entrance

Toilet

Butlers
Pantry

Study

Library

Panel Rm.

46'9"x23'8"

Hall

Ceiling 12'0"

Dining
Room
21'0"x35'0"
Ceiling 12'0"

Reception
Room

Guest
Chamber

Drawing
Room
21'0"x40'0"
Ceiling 12'0"

25'0"

67'6"

25'0"

The First Floor Plan of

𝔗𝔥𝔢 𝔙𝔞𝔫 ℜ𝔢𝔫𝔰𝔰𝔢𝔩𝔞𝔢𝔯 — 𝔐𝔞𝔫𝔬𝔯 𝔥𝔬𝔲𝔰𝔢 — 𝔄𝔩𝔟𝔞𝔫𝔶 — 𝔑𝔢𝔴 𝔜𝔬𝔯𝔨

graphic ～～～ scale

PAINTING of HOUSE made about 1830. This is the
only document in existence showing the original
character of the HOUSE before it was remodeled.

Mitchell Wooten Del.

203

East Elevati

Details of CENTRAL ARCH of
West Elevation showing carved
SPANDRELS taken from the book
of ornament by LOCK & COPELAND

North and South
graphic
Interior Details
of the Van Renss

The hand-painted, tempera WALL PAPER in the GREAT HAL
by PHILIP LIVINGSTON, the SIGNER, to his son-in-law, the

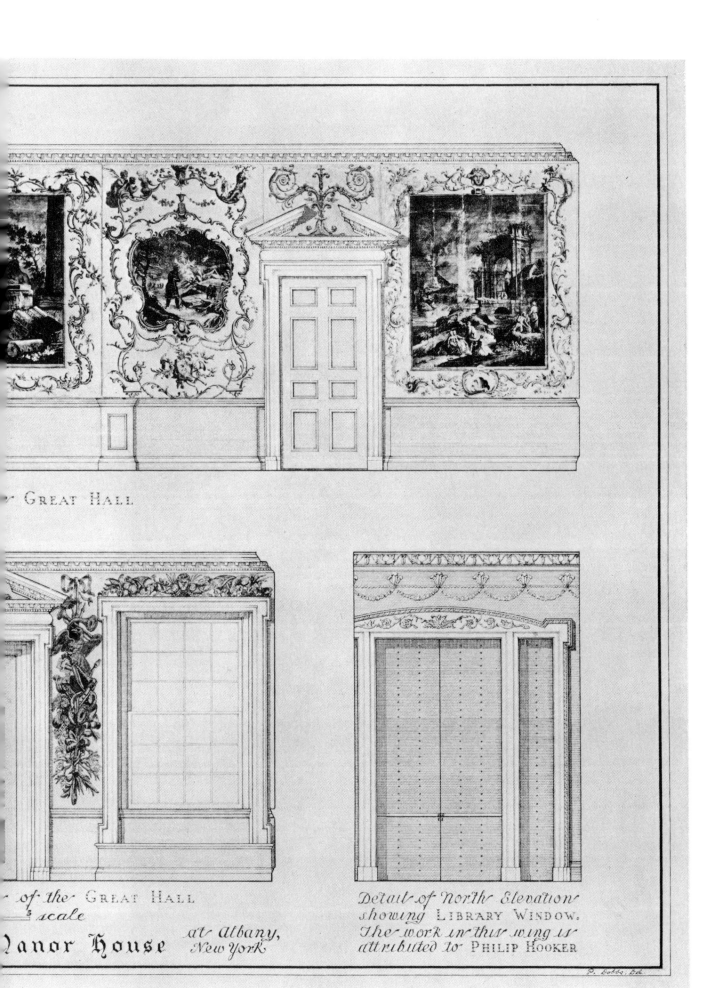

GREAT HALL

of the GREAT HALL
scale

Manor House at Albany, New York

Detail of North Elevation
showing LIBRARY WINDOW.
The work in this wing is
attributed to PHILIP HOOKER

P. Dobbs. Del.

made in England in 1768 by NEATE AND PIGOU, and sent
, STEPHEN VAN RENSSELAER. It cost £ 38..12..8½

Photograph by Edward Pierrepont Beckwith

SEPIA WATERCOLOR OF PHILIPSE MANOR HALL, SHOWING ITS SETTING IN 1754

SOUTH ELEVATION OF PHILIPSE MANOR HALL, YONKERS, NEW YORK

Photograph by Edward Pierrepont Beckwith

PHILIPSE MANOR HALL
YONKERS NEW YORK

Cornice Over
1st Story Windows

Section Through
Main Cornice

PHILIPSE MANOR HALL
WAS STARTED DURING THE
LAST HALF OF THE
SEVENTEENTH CENTURY
BY
FREDERICK PHILIPSE · MERCHANT AND
FIRST LORD OF THE MANOR
THE FAÇADE SHOWN IS PART OF THE
NORTH WING WHICH WAS ERECTED BY
FREDERICK PHILIPSE · SECOND LORD
ABOUT THE YEAR 1745

Cornice Over
The South Porch

Graphic Scale
Elevation
5 10 15 20 feet

Details
3 6 9 12 inches

E. H. Sammons Del.

208

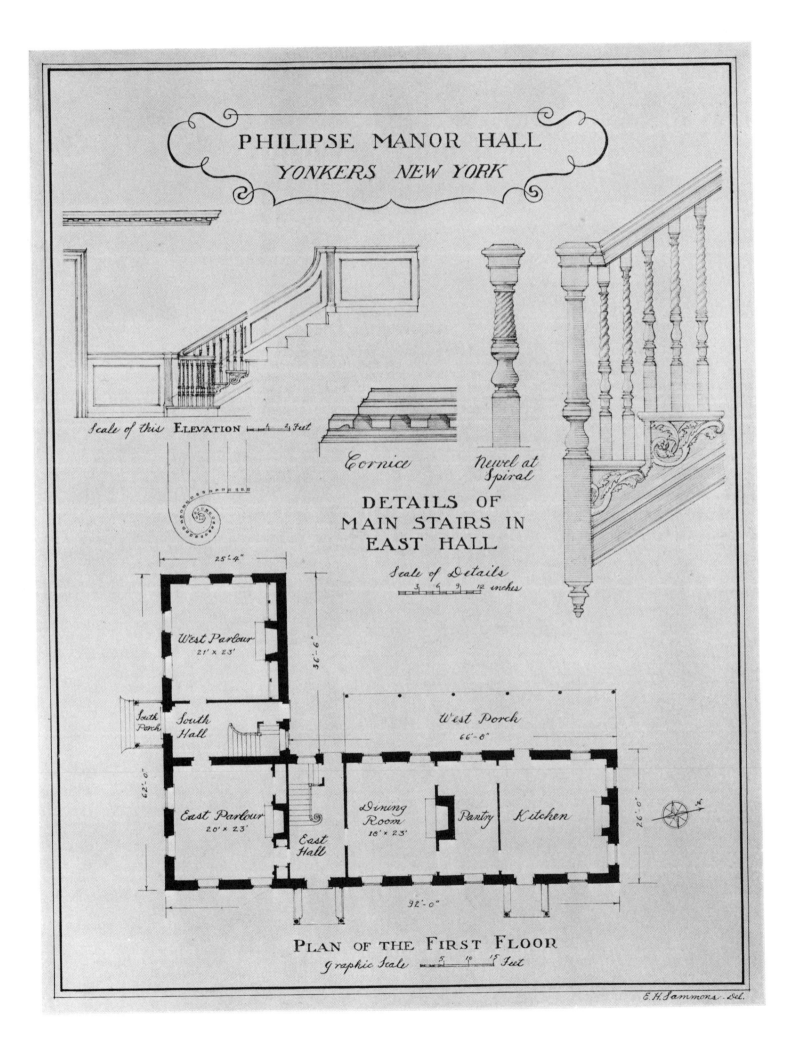

PHILIPSE MANOR HALL
YONKERS NEW YORK

Scale of this ELEVATION |⊢⊣| ¼ *Feet*

Cornice

Newel at Spiral

DETAILS OF MAIN STAIRS IN EAST HALL

Scale of Details |⊢⊣⊣⊣| 3 6 9 12 *inches*

25'-4"

36'-6"

62'-0"

26'-0"

West Parlour
21' x 23'

South Porch

South Hall

West Porch
66'-8"

East Parlour
20' x 23'

East Hall

Dining Room
18' x 23'

Pantry

Kitchen

92'-0"

PLAN OF THE FIRST FLOOR
Graphic Scale |⊢⊣⊣⊣| 5 10 15 *Feet*

E. H. Sammons. del.

The
EAST PARLOUR

PHILIPSE MANOR
HALL

YONKERS NEW YORK

Actual Scale 8'0"=3"
Details

Elevations

John Stacchetti Del.

Guest Chamber

Fireplace in West Parlour

PHILIPSE
MANOR
HALL
at
YONKERS NEW YORK
Scale
ELEVATIONS   DETAILS

E. H. Sammons, Del.

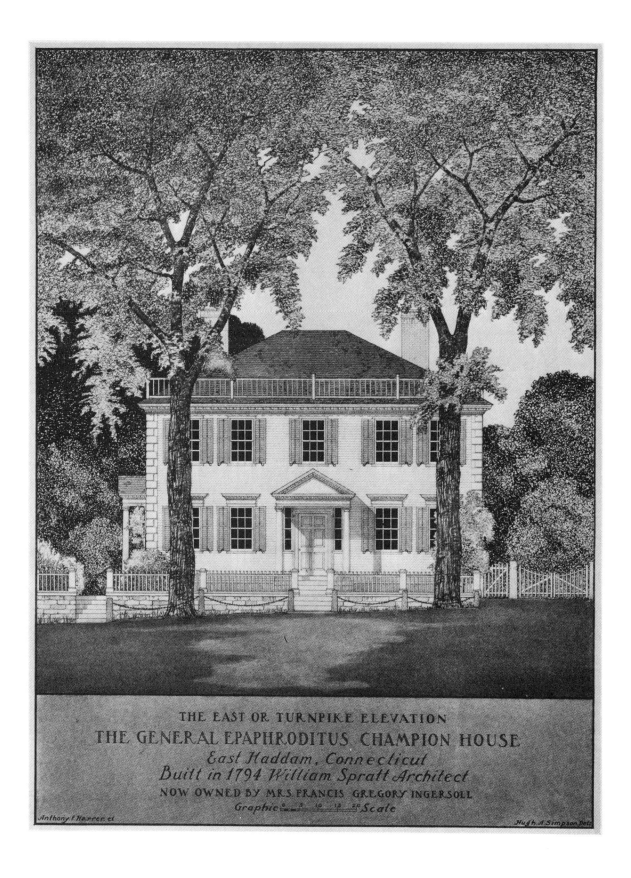

THE EAST OR TURNPIKE ELEVATION
THE GENERAL EPAPHRODITUS CHAMPION HOUSE
East Haddam, Connecticut
Built in 1794 William Spratt Architect
NOW OWNED BY MRS. FRANCIS GREGORY INGERSOLL
Graphic⁰ 5 10 15 20 Scale

Anthony F. Harren. el   Hugh A. Simpson Del.

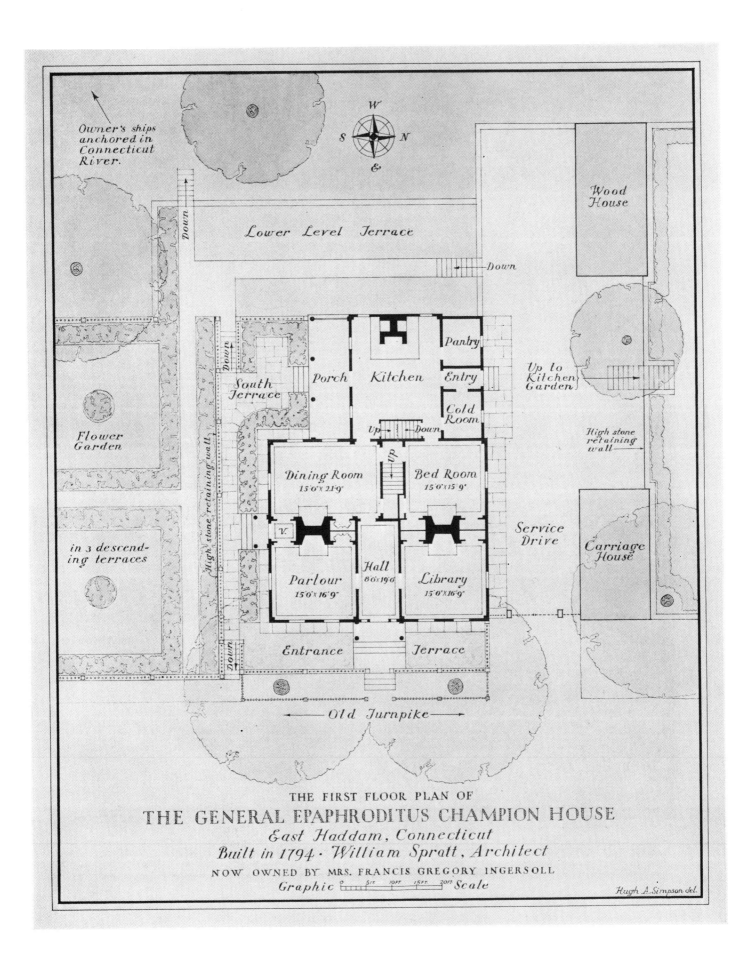

Owner's ships anchored in Connecticut River.

W S N &

Lower Level Terrace

Down

Down

Wood House

Up to Kitchen Garden

High stone retaining wall

South Terrace

Porch

Kitchen

Pantry

Entry

Cold Room

Flower Garden

Down

Up Down

Dining Room
15'0" x 21'9"

Up

Bed Room
15'0" x 15'9"

Service Drive

Carriage House

in 3 descending terraces

High stone retaining wall

V.

Hall
8'0" x 19'6"

Parlour
15'0" x 16'9"

Library
15'0" x 16'9"

Entrance

Terrace

← Old Turnpike →

THE FIRST FLOOR PLAN OF
THE GENERAL EPAPHRODITUS CHAMPION HOUSE
East Haddam, Connecticut
Built in 1794 · William Spratt, Architect
NOW OWNED BY MRS. FRANCIS GREGORY INGERSOLL
Graphic 0 5FT 10FT 15FT 20FT Scale

Hugh A. Simpson del.

GARDEN FAÇADE OF THE GENERAL EPAPHRODITUS CHAMPION HOUSE,
EAST HADDAM, CONNECTICUT

MANTEL AND OVERMANTEL OF THE PARLOUR OF THE
GENERAL EPAPHRODITUS CHAMPION HOUSE,
EAST HADDAM, CONNECTICUT

The wallpaper shown has a background of dead white with a pattern of rusty black
and gold. It is very rare and one of the earliest types of wallpaper

Front Elevation

Samuel Russell House

at Middletown Connecticut

Scale ▬ ▬ ▬ ▬ ▬ 16 Feet

Scale One Inch equals 16 Feet

GARDEN FAÇADE OF THE SAMUEL RUSSELL HOUSE, MIDDLETOWN, CONNECTICUT

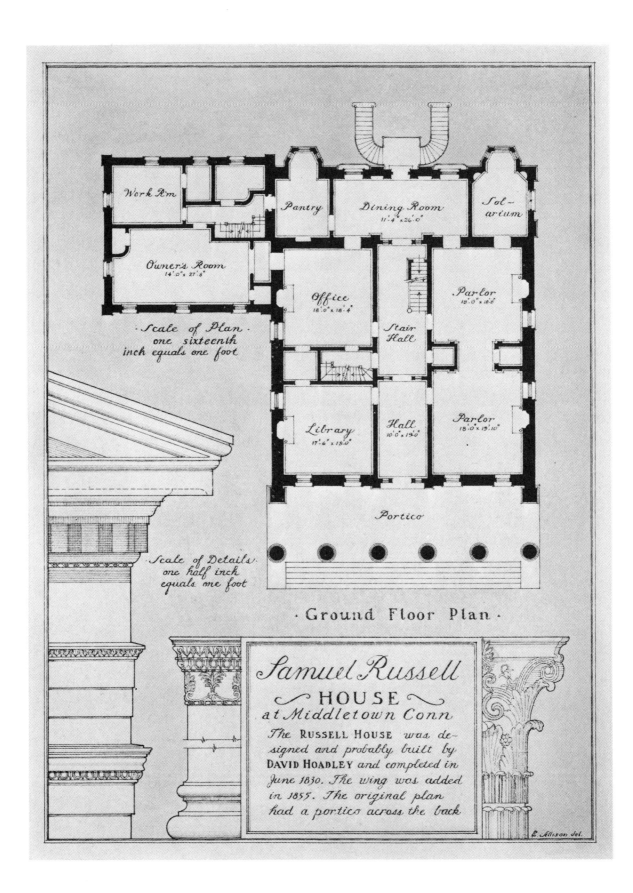

Work Rm

Pantry

Dining Room
11'4" x 26'0"

Sol-
arium

Owner's Room
14'0" x 27'5"

Office
18'0" x 18'4"

Stair
Hall

Parlor
18'0" x 18'8"

·Scale of Plan·
one sixteenth
inch equals one foot

Library
17'6" x 18'0"

Hall
10'0" x 19'0"

Parlor
18'0" x 19'10"

Scale of Details
one half inch
equals me foot

Portico

· Ground Floor Plan ·

Samuel Russell
HOUSE
at Middletown Conn

The RUSSELL HOUSE was de-
signed and probably built by
DAVID HOADLEY and completed in
June 1830. The wing was added
in 1855. The original plan
had a portico across the back

E. Allison del.

The West or Entrance Facade of
THE NIGHTINGALE HOUSE
357 Benefit Street Providence Rhode Is.
Built in 1792 by Colonel Joseph Nightingale
and attributed to Caleb Ormsbee Architect.
NOW THE HOME OF Mr. JOHN NICHOLAS BROWN
Graphic Scale

THE DOWNSTAIRS HALL OF THE NIGHTINGALE HOUSE, PROVIDENCE,
RHODE ISLAND

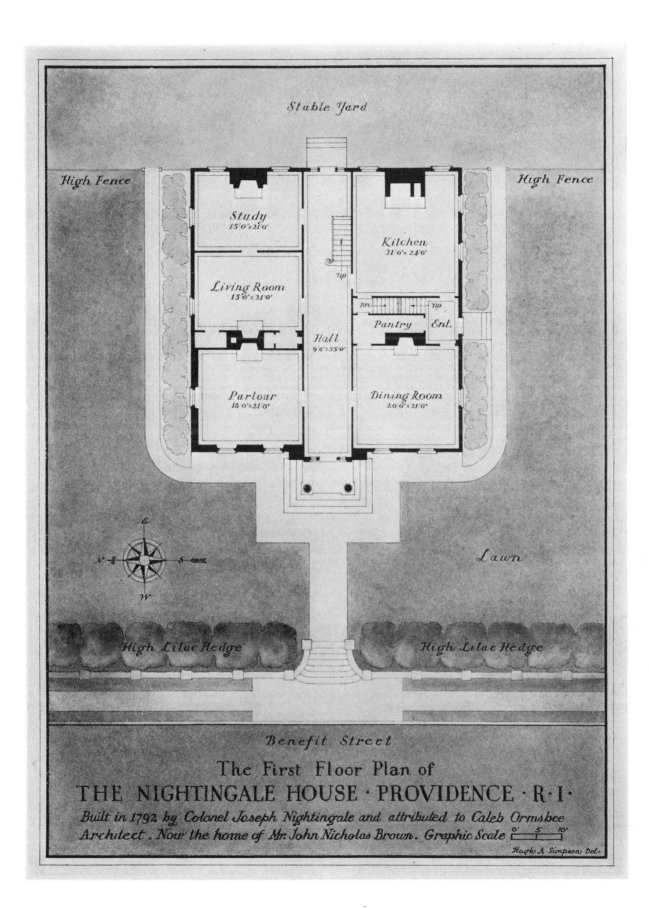

Stable Yard

High Fence

High Fence

Study
15'0"x21'0"

Kitchen
21'0"x24'0"

Living Room
15'0"x21'0"

up

dn   up

Pantry   Ent.

Hall
9'6"x55'0"

Parlour
18'0"x21'0"

Dining Room
20'0"x21'0"

Lawn

High Lilac Hedge

High Lilac Hedge

Benefit Street

The First Floor Plan of
THE NIGHTINGALE HOUSE · PROVIDENCE · R · I ·
Built in 1792 by Colonel Joseph Nightingale and attributed to Caleb Ormsbee
Architect. Now the home of Mr. John Nicholas Brown. Graphic Scale   0'   5'   10'

Hugh A. Simpson Del.

MANTEL AND OVERMANTEL OF THE STUDY OF THE NIGHTINGALE HOUSE,
PROVIDENCE, RHODE ISLAND

THE STUDY DOORWAY OF THE NIGHTINGALE HOUSE, PROVIDENCE,
RHODE ISLAND

The indication of busts of the mantelpiece and pediment is particularly interesting

ENTRANCE FAÇADE OF THE HARRISON GRAY OTIS HOUSE, 141 CAMBRIDGE
STREET, BOSTON, MASSACHUSETTS

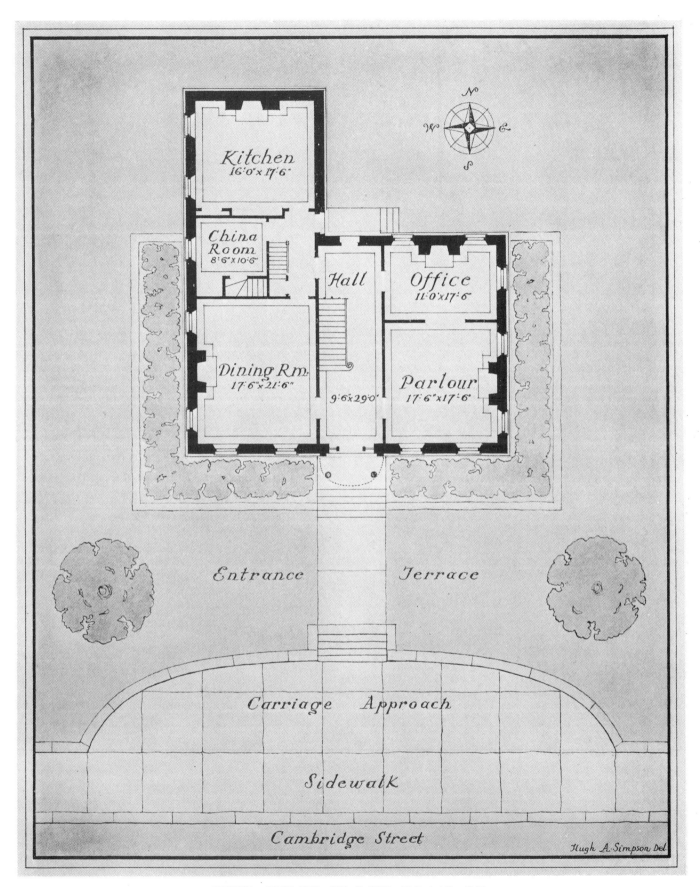

Kitchen
16'0" x 17'6"

China
Room
8'6" x 10'6"

Hall

Office
11'0" x 17'6"

Dining Rm.
17'6" x 21'6"

9'6" x 29'0"

Parlour
17'6" x 17'6"

Entrance   Terrace

Carriage   Approach

Sidewalk

Cambridge Street

Hugh A. Simpson Del.

THE FIRST FLOOR PLAN OF
THE HARRISON GRAY OTIS HOUSE
141 Cambridge Street Boston Massachusetts
Built in 1795. Charles Bulfinch, Architect
Now headquarters of the Society for the Preservation of New England Antiquities.
Graphic 0 FT. 5 FT. 10 FT. 15 FT. 20 FT. Scale

THE STAIR HALL OF THE HARRISON GRAY OTIS HOUSE, 141 CAMBRIDGE
STREET, BOSTON, MASSACHUSETTS

DINING ROOM DOORWAY OF THE HARRISON GRAY OTIS HOUSE,
141 CAMBRIDGE STREET, BOSTON, MASSACHUSETTS

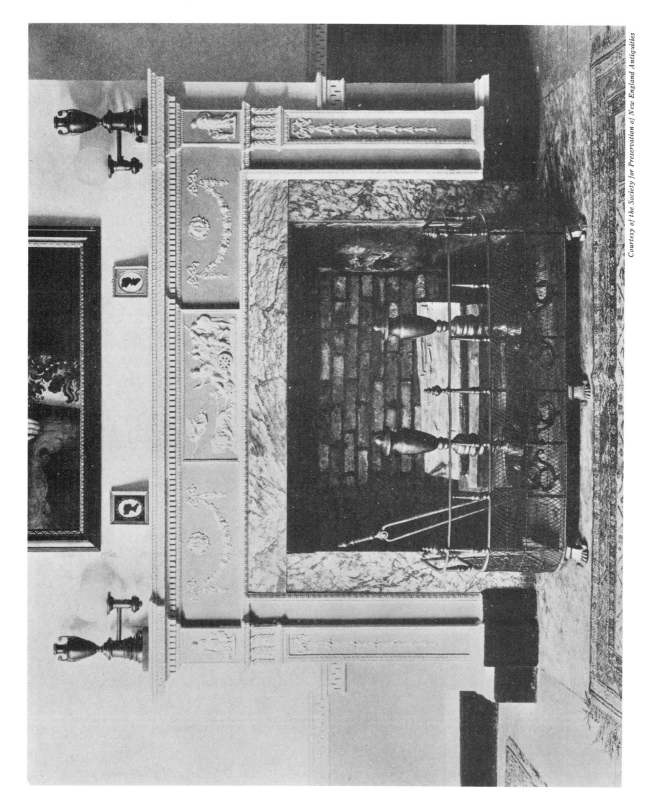

THE DINING ROOM MANTEL OF THE HARRISON GRAY OTIS HOUSE, 141 CAMBRIDGE STREET, BOSTON, MASSACHUSETTS

ENTRANCE FAÇADE OF THE HARRISON GRAY OTIS HOUSE, 45 BEACON STREET, BOSTON, MASSACHUSETTS

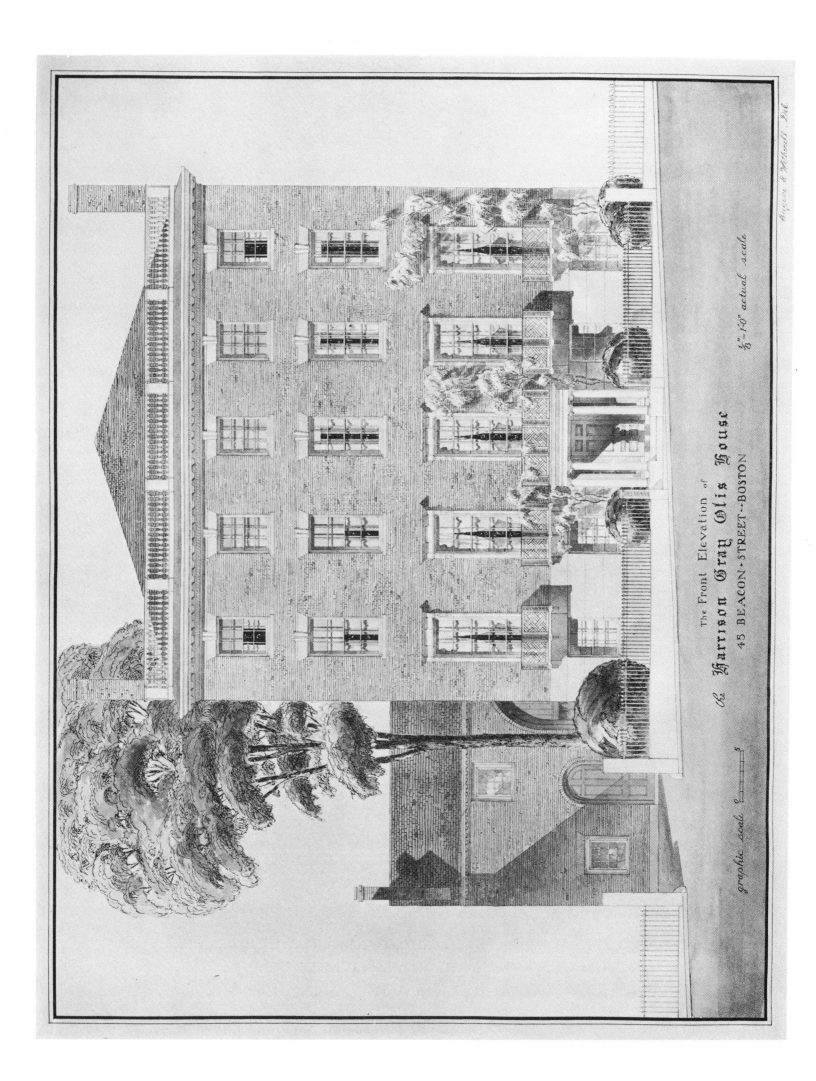

The Front Elevation of
The Harrison Gray Otis House
45 BEACON·STREET·BOSTON

graphic scale

⅛"=1'0" actual scale

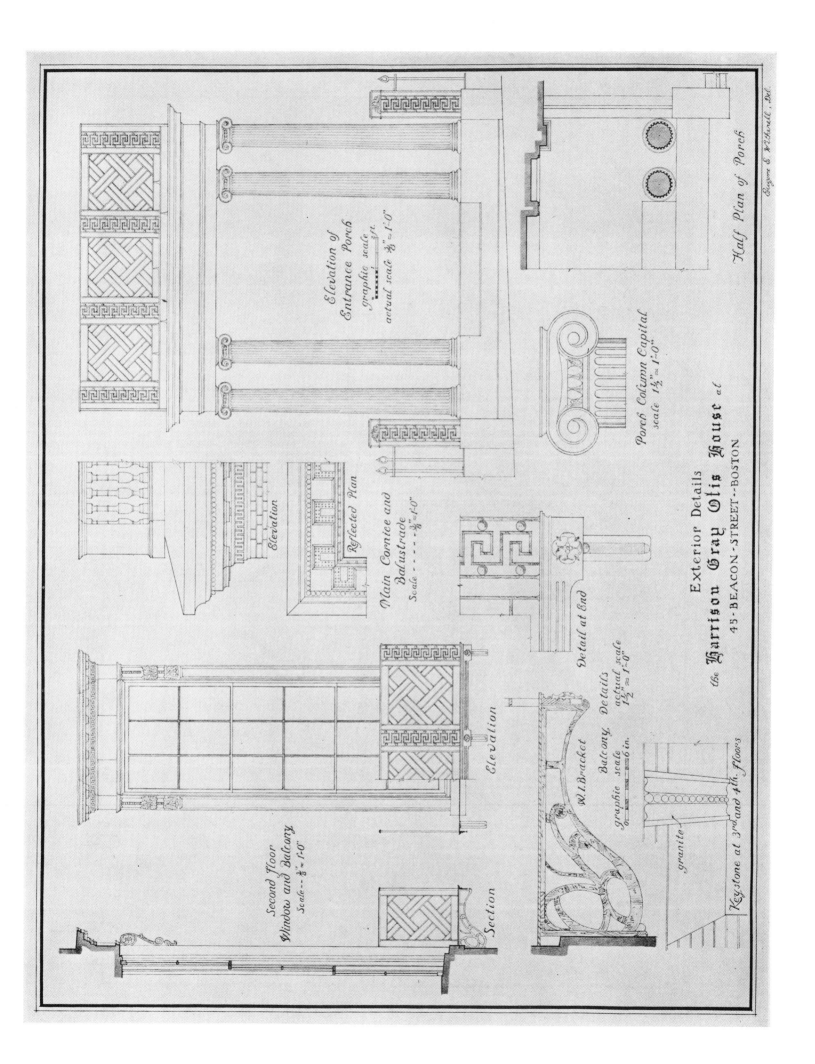

Elevation of
Entrance Porch
graphic scale
actual scale ½" = 1'-0"

Half Plan of Porch

Porch Column Capital
scale 1½" = 1'-0"

Elevation

Reflected Plan

Main Cornice and
Balustrade
Scale - - - - ½" = 1'-0"

Detail at End

Balcony Details
actual scale
1½" = 1'-0"

W. I. Bracket
graphic scale
0 6 in.

Keystone at 3rd and 4th Floors

granite

Second Floor
Window and Balcony
Scale - - ½" = 1'-0"

Elevation

Section

Exterior Details
the Harrison Gray Otis House at
45 - BEACON - STREET - BOSTON

Rogers & Witherell, Del.

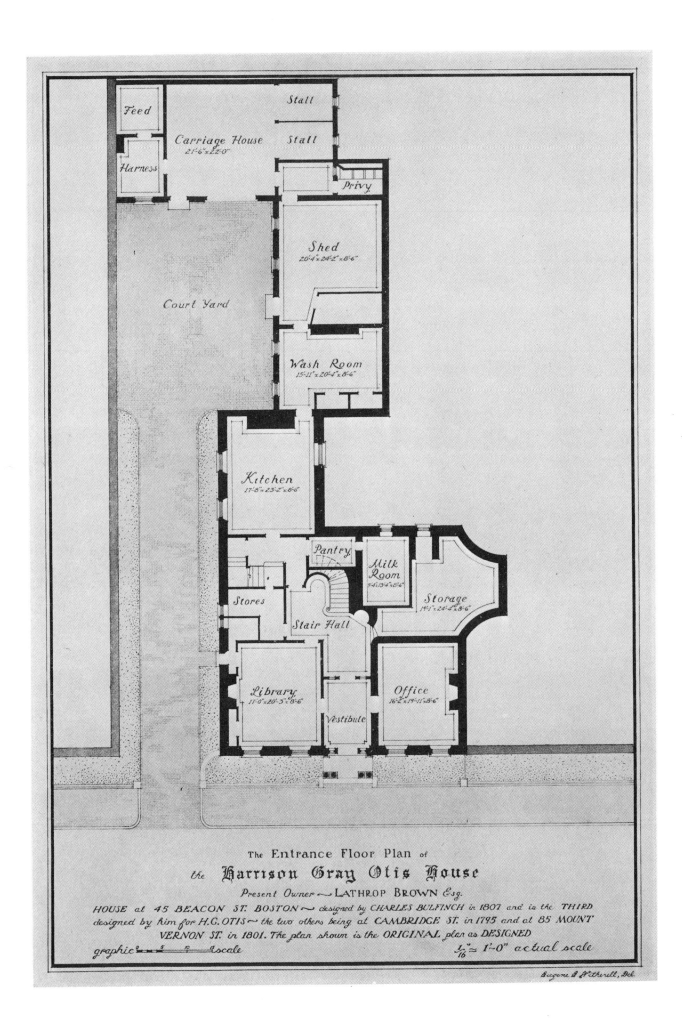

Feed

Stall

Carriage House
21'-6" x 22'-0"

Stall

Harness

Privy

Court Yard

Shed
20'-4" x 24'-2" x 8'-6"

Wash Room
15'-11" x 20'-4" x 8'-6"

Kitchen
17'-8" x 23'-2" x 8'-6"

Pantry

Milk
Room
9'-4" x 13'-4" x 8'-6"

Stores

Stair Hall

Storage
15'-1" x 24'-4" x 8'-6"

Library
17'-0" x 20'-5" x 8'-6"

Vestibule

Office
16'-2" x 19'-11" x 8'-6"

The Entrance Floor Plan of
the Harrison Gray Otis House
Present Owner — LATHROP BROWN Esq.
HOUSE at 45 BEACON ST. BOSTON — designed by CHARLES BULFINCH in 1807 and is the THIRD
designed by him for H.G. OTIS — the two others being at CAMBRIDGE ST. in 1795 and at 85 MOUNT
VERNON ST. in 1801. The plan shown is the ORIGINAL plan as DESIGNED
graphic ⊢——⊣ scale   1/16" = 1'-0" actual scale

Eugene A Wetherell, Del.

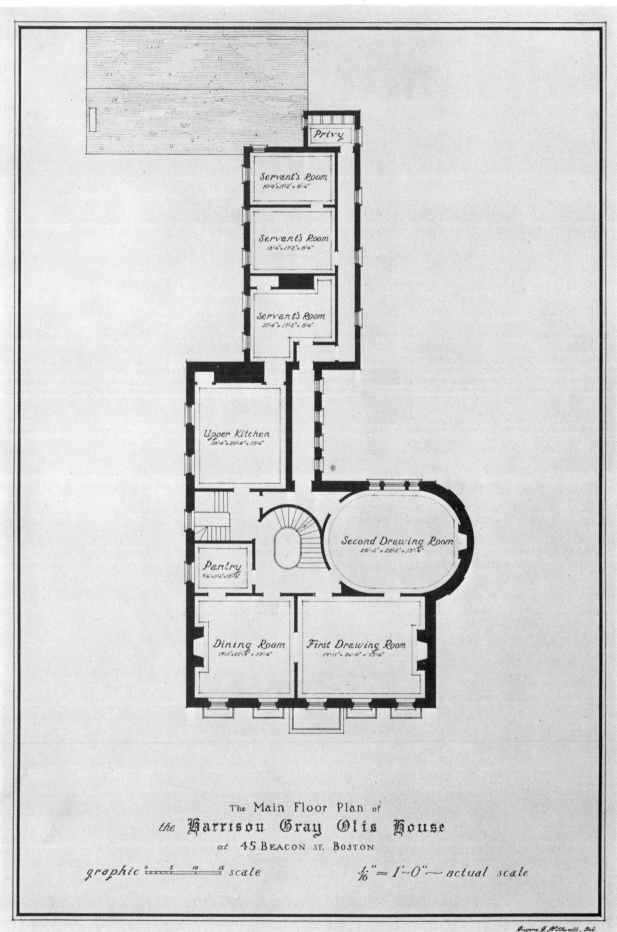

Privy

Servant's Room
10'-0" x 17'-2" x 8'-6"

Servant's Room
13'-6" x 17'-2" x 8'-6"

Servant's Room
10'-4" x 17'-2" x 8'-6"

Upper Kitchen
18'-4" x 20'-8" x 13'-6"

Second Drawing Room
20'-2" x 28'-2" x 13'-6"

Pantry
9'-6" x 11'-6" x 13'-6"

Dining Room
19'-1" x 20'-9" x 13'-6"

First Drawing Room
19'-11" x 26'-0" x 13'-6"

The Main Floor Plan of
the Harrison Gray Otis House
at 45 Beacon st. Boston

graphic ⊢——┼——┤ scale
         5   10   15

$\frac{1}{16}$" = 1'-0" — actual scale

Eugene C. Hitchell, Del.

→ THE · DRIV
THE · GOVERN
OLD · ALBANY · POST · RO
Built in 1805~
Graphic

ACADE · OF ·
GORE · HOUSE ·
THAM · MASSACHUSETTS
lfinch ~ Architect
20
Scale

Wallace Heath del.

THE GARDEN FAÇADE OF THE GOVERNOR GORE HOUSE, OLD ALBANY POST ROAD, WALTHAM, MASSACHUSETTS. NOW THE PROPERTY OF THE WALTHAM GOLF CLUB

South Lawn

Kitchen
17'·6"·19'·5"

Services
9'·2"·37'·5"

Pantry

Family
Dining Room
17'·0"·20'·0"

Drawing Room
26'·0"·30'·0"

Parlor
14'·6"·19'·0"

State
Dining Room
20'·6"·30'·0"

Stair
Hall

Hall
14'·4"·17'·0"

Billiard Room
18'·3"·30'·0"

Library
17'·4"·19'·6"

Entrance Terrace

Drive way

·THE·FIRST·FLOOR·PLAN·OF·
·THE·GOVERNOR·GORE·HOUSE·
OLD·ALBANY·POST·ROAD~WALTHAM·MASSACHUSETTS
·Built in 1805~ Charles Bulfinch·Architect·

237

ENTRANCE FAÇADE OF THE THEODORE LYMAN HOUSE, WALTHAM, MASSACHUSETTS

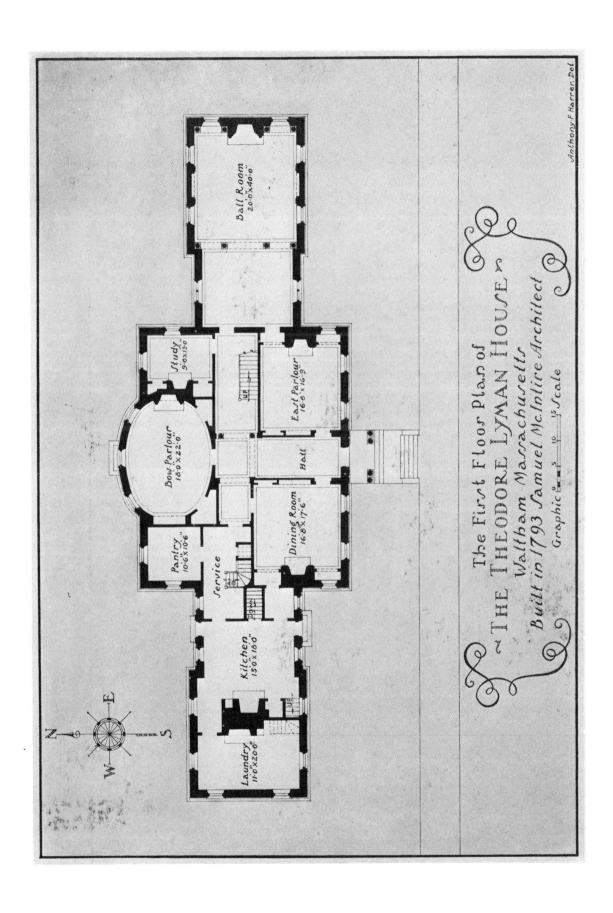

Ball Room
20'-0"x40'-0"

Study
9'-0"x13'-0"

Bow Parlour
18'-0"x22'-0"

UP

East Parlour
16'-8"x16'-9"

Pantry
10'-6"x10'-6"

Service

Hall

Dining Room
16'-8"x17'-6"

DOWN

Kitchen
15'-0"x18'-0"

UP

Laundry
11'-0"x20'-0"

N E S W

Anthony F Harrer Del.

The First Floor Plan of
~ THE THEODORE LYMAN HOUSE ~
Waltham Massachusetts
Built in 1793 Samuel McIntire Architect

Graphic Scale

239

Photograph by Paul J. Weber

DETAILS OF THE EAST END OF THE BALLROOM OF THE THEODORE
LYMAN HOUSE, WALTHAM, MASSACHUSETTS

ENTRANCE FAÇADE OF THE JEREMIAH LEE MANSION, MARBLEHEAD,
MASSACHUSETTS

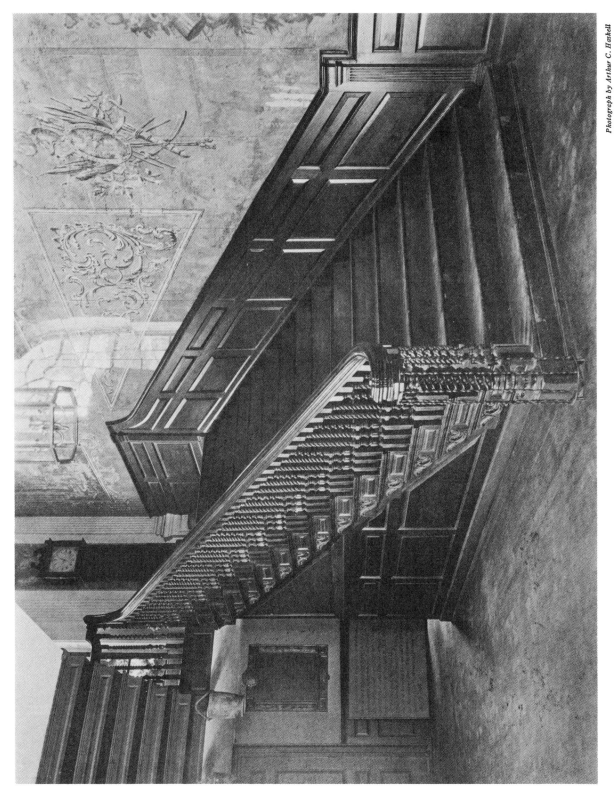

DETAIL OF THE MAIN STAIRWAY OF THE JEREMIAH LEE MANSION, MARBLEHEAD,
MASSACHUSETTS, SHOWING THE HAND PAINTED ENGLISH GEORGIAN WALLPAPER

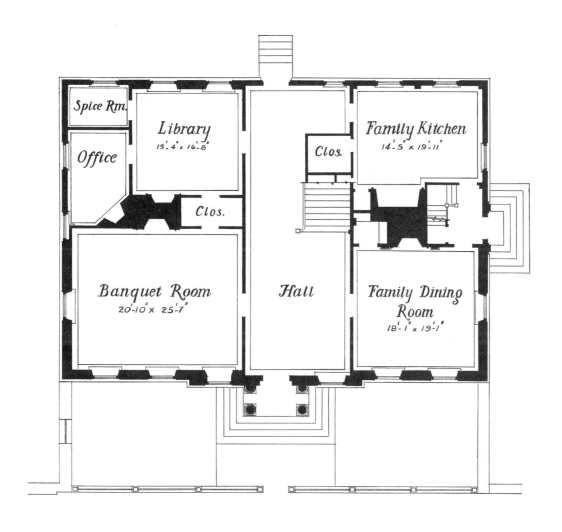

First Floor Plan

Jeremiah Lee Mansion
Marblehead Mass.

Scale ▬▬▬▬ 10 Feet

Photograph by Arthur G. Haskell

DETAIL OF THE HAND PAINTED ENGLISH GEORGIAN WALLPAPER
OF THE STAIR HALL OF THE JEREMIAH LEE MANSION,
MARBLEHEAD, MASSACHUSETTS

DETAIL OF THE MANTELPIECE IN THE BANQUETTING ROOM OF THE
JEREMIAH LEE MANSION, MARBLEHEAD, MASSACHUSETTS. THE
DESIGN WAS TAKEN FROM SWAN'S "BRITISH ARCHITECT," OF 1745

The Entrance Facade of
GRASSE·MOUNT ~ BURLINGTON ~ VERMONT
Built in 1804 by Captain Thaddeus Tuttle.
Now owned by The University of Vermont.
Graphic Scale

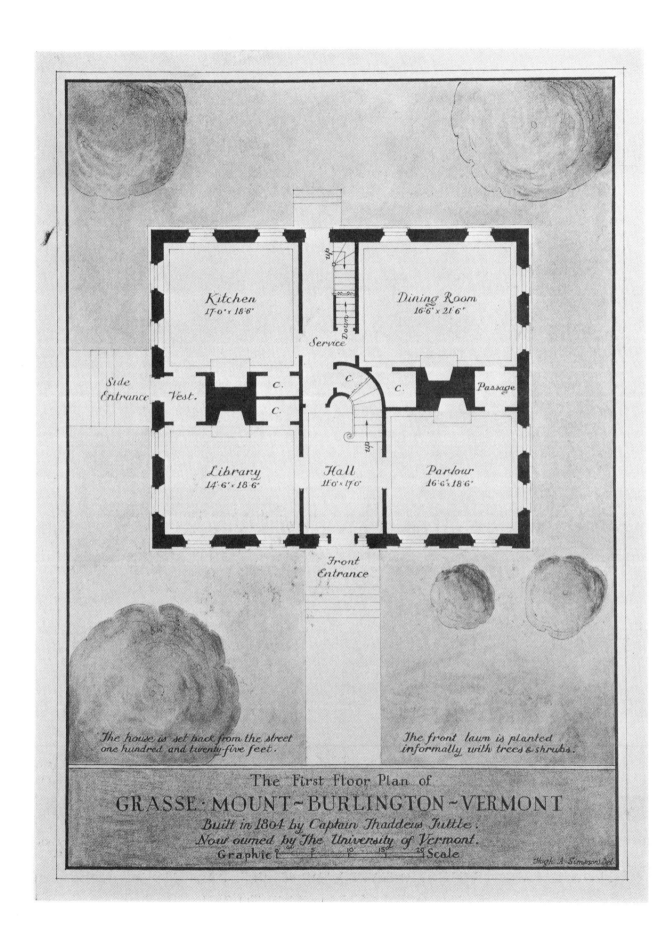

Kitchen
17'·0" x 18'·6"

Dining Room
16'·6" x 21'·6"

Service

Down

Side
Entrance

Vest.

C.

C.

C.

C.

Passage

Library
14'·6" x 18'·6"

Hall
11'·0" x 17'·0"

Up

Parlour
16'·6" x 18'·6"

Front
Entrance

The house is set back from the street
one hundred and twenty-five feet.

The front lawn is planted
informally with trees & shrubs.

The First Floor Plan of

GRASSE·MOUNT ~ BURLINGTON ~ VERMONT

Built in 1804 by Captain Thaddeus Tuttle.
Now owned by The University of Vermont.

Graphic   5   10   15   20   Scale

Hugh A. Simpson Del.

MAIN FAÇADE OF THE MOFFATT-LADD HOUSE, PORTSMOUTH, NEW
HAMPSHIRE, SHOWING THE OFFICE TO THE RIGHT

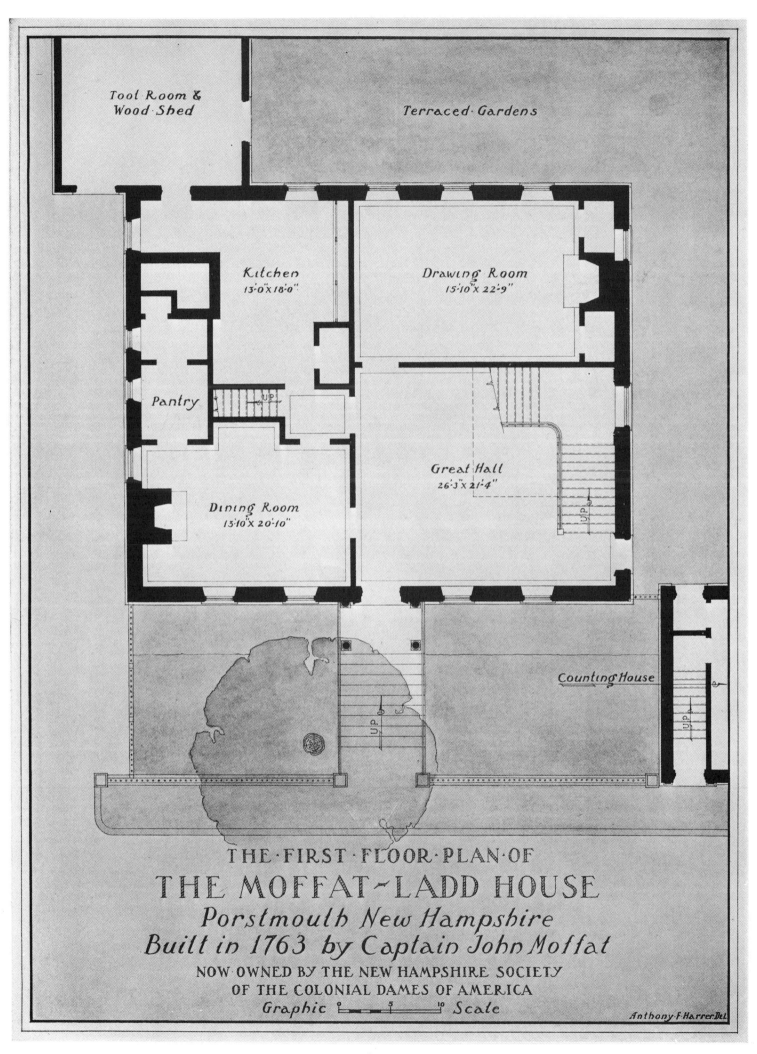

Tool Room &
Wood Shed

Terraced Gardens

Kitchen
13'-0" x 18'-0"

Drawing Room
15'-10" x 22'-9"

Pantry

Great Hall
26'-3" x 21'-4"

Dining Room
13'-10" x 20'-10"

UP

UP

UP

Counting House

UP

THE·FIRST·FLOOR·PLAN·OF
THE MOFFAT~LADD HOUSE
Porstmouth New Hampshire
Built in 1763 by Captain John Moffat
NOW·OWNED BY THE NEW HAMPSHIRE SOCIETY
OF THE COLONIAL DAMES OF AMERICA
Graphic ├──┼──┤ Scale

Anthony F Harrer Del.

STAIR HALL OF THE MOFFATT-LADD HOUSE, PORTSMOUTH, NEW HAMPSHIRE

DETAIL OF THE DRAWING ROOM MANTELPIECE OF THE MOFFATT-LADD HOUSE,
PORTSMOUTH, NEW HAMPSHIRE

Front Elevation

McPhedrisᐧWarner House

PORTSMOUTH · · NEW · HAMPSHIRE

Actual Scale
⅛" = 1'-0"

Graphic Scale

Philo Sargillgoo.Del

ENTRANCE FAÇADE

This, the oldest brick house in the city of Portsmouth, was built in the years between 1718 and 1723 at a cost of six thousand pounds by Captain McPhedris, a native of Scotland, a member of the King's Council, and a wealthy merchant. The walls, eighteen inches thick, are constructed of brick brought from Holland as were some of the other building materials. Captain McPhedris was married to Miss Sarah Wentworth, daughter of Governor John Wentworth. Their daughter Mary married the Honorable Jonathan Warner. Their name has thus become identified with this mansion.

At the time of its building it was scarcely surpassed by any private residence in New England.

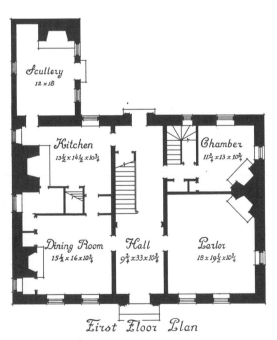

Scullery
12 x 18

Kitchen
13½ x 14½ x 10¾

Chamber
11¾ x 13 x 10¾

Dining Room
15½ x 16 x 10¾

Hall
9¾ x 33 x 10¾

Parlor
18 x 19½ x 10¾

First Floor Plan

Graphic Scale
0   10   20

McPhedris-Warner House
PORTSMOUTH · · NEW · HAMPSHIRE

Actual Scale
1/16" ≈ 1'-0"
Eugene E. Witherell, Del.

The
**Mc Phedris-
Warner
House**
in
PORTSMOUTH
NEW · HAMPSHIRE
1718 ~ 1723

*Upon the walls of the
hall there are various
paintings by unknown
artists - a life-size portrait of Governor Phipps
on horseback, a woman
spinning, her work in-
terrupted by a hawk
lighting among the chick-
ens and a Biblical scene
of Abraham offering
up Isaac. On the spaces
at either side of the window on the stair land-
ing are life-size figures
of Indians, supposedly
portraits of aborigines
with whom the original
owner had traded.*

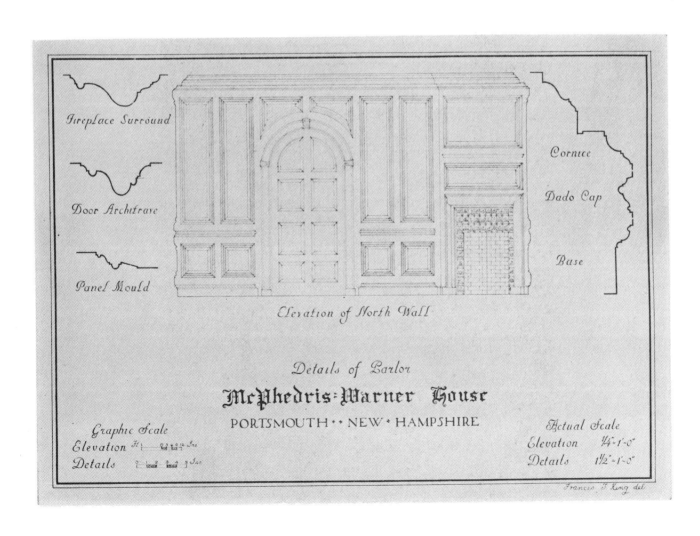

Fireplace Surround

Door Architrave

Panel Mould

Cornice

Dado Cap

Base

Elevation of North Wall

Details of Parlor

McPhedris-Warner House

PORTSMOUTH · · NEW · HAMPSHIRE

Graphic Scale
Elevation Ft.
Details

Actual Scale
Elevation ¼"=1'-0"
Details 1½"=1'-0"

Francis T. King del.

255

ENTRANCE FAÇADE OF THE LADY PEPPERELL HOUSE, KITTERY POINT, MAINE

East Entrance Facade

The Lady Pepperell House ~ Kittery Point ~ Maine

Built by or for LADY PEPPERELL shortly after the death of SIR WILLIAM in 1759
some say as a DOWER HOVSE ~ This house is said to have been connected by a vast double
row of elms with the PEPPERELL MANSION which stood in its own DEER PARK

Scale feet 1 2 3 4 8

J. Howells. del.

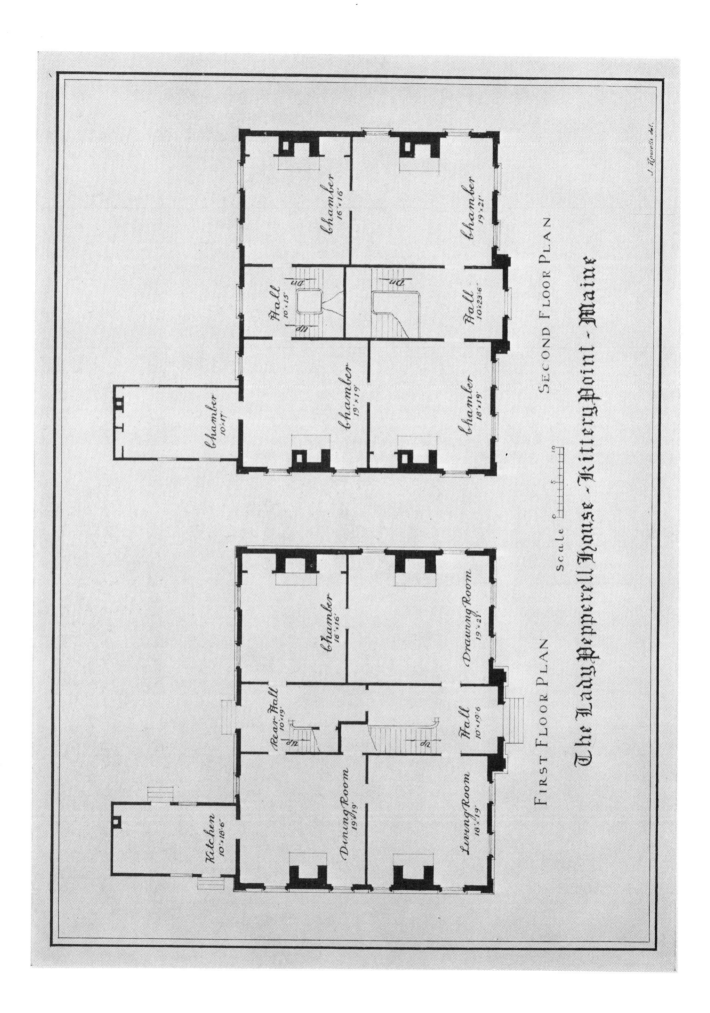

J. Howells del.

FIRST FLOOR PLAN

SECOND FLOOR PLAN

Scale

The Lady Pepperell House - Kittery Point - Maine

258

THE STAIR HALL OF THE LADY PEPPERELL HOUSE,
KITTERY POINT, MAINE

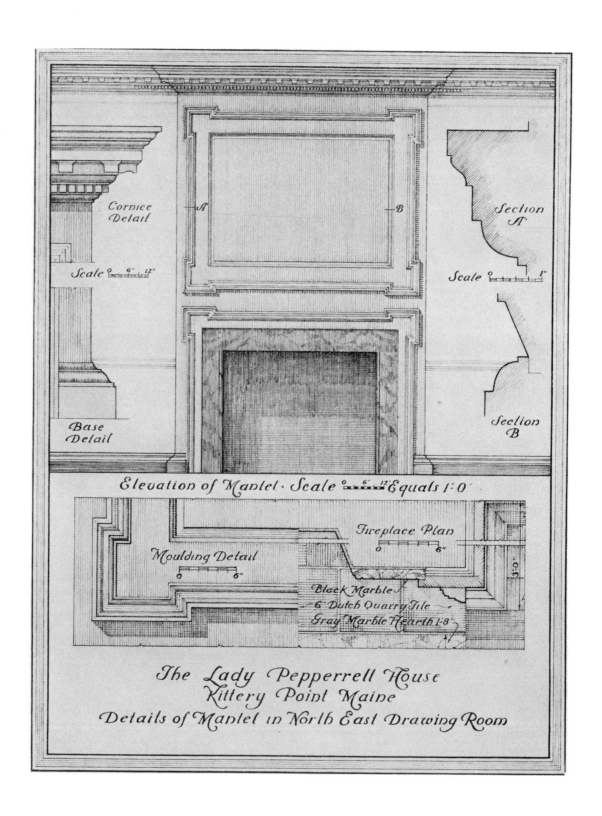

Cornice Detail

A   B

Section A

Scale 0 6" 12"

Scale 0 1"

Base Detail

Section B

Elevation of Mantel · Scale 0 6" 12" Equals 1'·0"

Moulding Detail

Fireplace Plan

6"

3'·0"

6"

Black Marble
6 Dutch Quarry Tile
Gray Marble Hearth 1·8"

The Lady Pepperrell House
Kittery Point Maine
Details of Mantel in North East Drawing Room

DETAIL OF THE ENTRANCE OF THE McLENNAN-SWEAT HOUSE,
PORTLAND, MAINE, NOW THE L. D. M. SWEAT
MEMORIAL ART MUSEUM

Scale for Elevation

0   5   10   20   30   40FT

Detail of
Entrance Doorway

Scale For Details

0   1   2   3   4   5FT.

The McLennan - Sweat House, PORTLAND, MAINE

Built in 1800 by HUGH McLENNAN. ALEXANDER PARRIS Architect
Shortly after completion, due to financial reverses, the ownership was relinquished.
Acquired by General JOSHUA WINGATE who owned it until about 1855, passed into hands of
CHAS CLAPP bought by LORENZO di MEDICI SWEAT in 1880. In 1908 willed to city as a memorial.

Entrance Under Stair Landing

0 1 2 3 4 5 FT.

Library
11'-0" x 16'-8"

Kitchen
15'-6" x 18'-0"

Living Rm
16'-8" x 28'-6"

Hall
12'-6" x 39'-6"

Dining Rm
18'-0" x 20'-6"

· First · Floor · Plan ·

0 5 10 20 30 40 FT.

Mc Lennan · Sweat House

PORTLAND, MAINE

ALEXANDER PARRIS Architect

Paul S. Singer del.

Section Thru Stair Hall

0   5   10   15 FT.

Scale for Section

At Left 2nd Fl. Doorway

At Right 1st Fl. Doorway

Stair Detail

Scale for Details

0   1   2   3   4 FT.

Mc Lennan · Sweat House
PORTLAND, MAINE
ALEXANDER PARRIS Architect.

Paul d Staor del